TOY AUTOS

1890-1939

NEW CAVENDISH BOOKS

Dedicated to the memory of
Peter Ottenheimer

Principal Consultant: *David Pressland*
Text Consultant: *Michelle Lovric*

Editor: Allen Levy
German translation: *Michael Roesen*
French translation: *Chantal le Vaillant de Folleville/Monelle Hayot*
Research: *Justin Knowles/David Pressland*
Photography: *Graham Strong/assisted by Nick Daly*
Backgrounds: *Tony Strong Associates/concepts by Graham Strong*
Design: *Roger Huggett/Supadee Ruangsak*

Printed in China under the supervision of
Mandarin Offset London

New Cavendish Books Ltd.
3 Denbigh Road
London W11 2SJ

ISBN 1 872727 61 1

C O N T E N T S

FOREWORD

The development of the 'horseless carriage', as virtually all the great technological advances (of the last century in particular), was mirrored by toymakers throughout the period.

Whereas railways were subjected to the scrutiny of model enthusiasts and a market requiring scale appearance early in their history, road vehicles retained that element of whimsy well into the early 1930s until the advent of small diecast toys.

It is also a fact that far more people came into contact with railways and public motor vehicles than private cars in the first decades of the twentieth century. The dates of this work, 1890-1939 coincides with an era of relative innocence and naivety, in the fashioning of toy motor vehicles – if little else. A casual browse through the rich imagery that follows will reinforce the view that toy autos of this period now bear all the hallmarks of the folk art that grew out of the emerging love affair with the car and all its derivatives.

The toy vehicles illustrated in this book are largely drawn from one of the great post-war collections which sadly has now been dispersed. This approach has the singular advantage of presenting the reader with the best examples in both terms of condition and interlocking relevance. The hallmark of any great toy collection is the constant upgrading and sourcing of items to give balance in terms of makers both obscure and famous. In this case such connoisseurship reflects the change of style from the horse-drawn coach appearance of the first vehicles to the wonderfully overstyled monsters of the 1930s.

As with so many commercial artefacts of the last century, national characteristics may be observed. Germany was the hub of invention and production methods and few toys have surpassed the pure quality of early hand- enamelled

vehicles by Bing and the somewhat rarer examples by Marklin. While hand-painted cars from France exhibited a similar artistic licence, it was not until the 1920s that French makers, particularly JEP and Rossignol, produced toy cars that truly rivalled their German counterparts. In Britain toy vehicles (often derived from former German tooling) were produced at various times to satisfy the 'buy British' fever which understandably gripped the nation after the First World War. Curiously this mood was less marked in the aftermath of 1945.

The catalogue reproductions covering two key periods of this book illustrate the exaggerated and stylised designs created by one maker to attract the young and no doubt not so young buyers of the time. Many theories could be advanced as to which real life cars are depicted. Perhaps the best toys as distinct from models are ones where the toymaker's vision is unclouded by reality.

Virtually all this industry moved to the Far East in the 1950s. Japanese-made toy cars of the fifties and beyond were to become as collectable (and in some instances as valuable) as their European forebears, but that, as they say, 'is another story'. Nonetheless the toy autos that sparkle on these pages represent a time of wonder that is no more. In retrospect that time was incredibly brief and in some ways represented a fusion of art and commerce that occurs as if by accident. Doubtless future historians might reflect on the imagery of the tin toy autos in this book with other considered icons of the machine age.

On a personal note I can't help feeling that the tin art depicted here will be a rich source of material for future generations. It was after all a bustling part of the view through a child's window on to the twentieth century.

Allen Levy
London 1993

New fine Models of modern Motor Cars

very elegantly finished, with **extra strong, best quality clockwork,** pneumatic rubber tyres, **plastic seats** (imitation cushions), cooling box in fine brass finish and brake; front axle adjustable to **run straight** or **in a circle,** with lanterns

13657

13659

13657	$9^7/_8$ in. long, $4^1/_2$ in. wide, $4^1/_8$ in. high	each	**12/8**
13658	$11^1/_2$ „ „ $5^1/_8$ „ „ $5^1/_8$ „ „	„	**20/—**

13659 very elegant finish with finely nickelled **head light** for **real burning**

$13^3/_4$ in. long, $6^1/_4$ in. wide, $6^1/_4$ in. high . . . . each **28/2**

13660/0   13660/1 and 2

Motor Racing Cars,

finest finish with **extra strong, best quality** clockwork, pneumatic rubber tyres, and **reserve tyre,** with real cushions on the seats, cooling box in fine brass finish and brake; front axle adjustable to run straight or in a circle.

13660/0	$8^1/_4$ in. long, $4^3/_8$ in. wide, 4 in. high	each	**9/8**
„ /1	$11^1/_2$ „ „ $4^3/_8$ „ „ $4^3/_4$ „ „	„	**13/—**
„ /2	$15^3/_8$ „ „ $5^1/_2$ „ „ $6^3/_8$ „ „	„	**24/—**

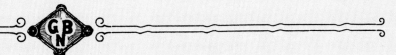

New fine Models of modern Motor Cars

very elegantly finished, with **extra strong, best quality clockwork**, pneumatic rubber tyres, **plastic seats** (imitation cushions), cooling box in fine brass finish and brake; front axle adjustable to **run straight** or in **a circle,** with lanterns and doors to open

14126/1   **14126/2**

14126/1 Cab (Coupé) with 1 Lantern, $7^7/_8$ in. long, 4 in. wide, $4^3/_4$ in. high . . . . each **13/10**
„ /2 „ „ „ 2 „ $8^1/_4$ „ 5 „ $5^1/_8$ „ „ . . . . „ **17/10**

14150/1   **14150/2**

14150/1 Touring Car with 1 Lantern, $8^1/_4$ in. long, $4^1/_8$ in. wide, $5^1/_8$ in. high . . . . . . each **15/10**
„ /2 „ „ „ 2 „ 9 „ „ $4^3/_4$ „ $5^7/_8$ „ „ . . . . . . „ **20/4**

14001/1   **14001/2**

14001/1 Break with hooter sounding "Tuff-Tuff" $8^1/_4$ in. long, $4^1/_8$ in. wide, 4 in. high . . each **12/4**
„ /2 „ „ „ „ „ $9^1/_2$ „ „ $5^1/_8$ „ „ $4^1/_2$ „ „ . . „ **16/8**
„ /3 „ „ „ „ „ 11 „ „ $5^7/_8$ „ „ $5^3/_4$ „ „ . . „ **25/10**

PRINCIPAL MANUFACTURERS OF TIN TOY CARS

Numbers after each entry refer to the pages on which the toys appear.

ANDRÉ, D.

No reference to this maker other than they made a series of cheap tin toys in the Marseille area has been established.
165

BING

Founded in 1866 at Nuremberg (the centre of the German toy manufacturing industry) by Ignatius and Adolf Bing, the company was in existence until 1933, when it was taken over by Karl Bub. By then it had achieved a world market. Bing cars are full of fine detail and ingenuity, often combining fantasy of a high order with mechanical precision and inventiveness. Its trademarks include 'GBN' (Gebruder Bing Nurnberg) and 'BW' (Bing Werke).
16, 36, 44-47, 54-57, 59-61, 74-75, 89, 96, 122-124, 162-163

BRIMTOY

Formed in 1923 this firm made a large range of tin toys some of which were derived from German maker's tooling some acquired via reparations following the first world war. In 1932 the company was absorbed by Wells o' London.

BUB

Founded by Karl Bub at Nuremberg in 1851, this firm began to produce toy cars in the 1920s. The cars have good detail, and often feature metal wheels with fine lithography. The company took over the Bing Company in 1933, and survived until 1964. Its trademarks include 'KBN' (Karl Bub Nurnberg), and 'KB'.
42, 71-73, 81, 118-120, 124-127, 129, 152-155, 163

BURNETT

A British firm, Burnett's trademark was a device incorporating St.George of England. Registered in 1914, the company was taken over by Chad Valley in the 1940s. This firm was responsible for some of the best lithographed toys made in Britain, in particular buses and vans.
70-71, 92, 135

CARDINI

This Italian company was founded at Omegna in 1922. Its vehicles were usually somewhat small, and there were five main lines. The finish of the cars is of high quality. An interesting feature is the box in which they were offered for sale; it could be transformed into a

garage, equipped with personnel. The company went out of business in 1928. The cars bore a large Cardini crest and wheels marked 'Pirelli-cord'.
119

CARETTE

Another major Nuremberg firm, founded in 1886 by Georges Carette; it went out of business in 1917. Carette cars are of excellent quality and are notable for their fine spoked wheels and distinctively shaped headlights. There were four major Carette trademarks varying by period, each incorporating the initials 'GC'.
33, 38, 43, 51-53, 59, 62-63

CHAD VALLEY

This British company was founded in 1823 and until 1980 produced a wide range of toys and games. The manufacture of tinplate cars began shortly after the Second World War. Its range also included construction-kit model cars developed from the Burnett line The firm's products carry the name of the firm in plain lettering often with a Royal Coat of Arms.
166

CITROEN

This French company produced toy cars from 1923. They were trademarked with a stencilled motif incorporating the name André Citroen.Initially these toys were manufactured for Citroen by Fabrique de Jeux Jouets later CIJ (1922-1934). Later models were made by JRD notably the immortal 'Traction' models.
128

DISTLER

The company was founded by Johann Distler in Nuremberg at the end of the nineteenth century. Distler went out of business in 1962. Pre-war models carry either the thistle trademark or the monogram 'JD'; postwar toys simply the name 'Distler'.
121, 150, 164

DOLL ET CIE

Founded at Nuremberg in 1898 by J Sondheim and Peter Doll, the company specialised in the production of various types of stationary steam engines and accessories. The company was taken over by Fleischmann in the late 1930s but the Doll name was retained until the early postwar period. The trademark was based on the initials 'DC'.
124, 151

EBERL

H E N was the trade mark of Hans Eberl, a Nuremburg toy firm that does not appear to have survived the First World War. Their toy cars in particular exhibited extremely rich lithography.
41, 56-57

FISCHER

H Fischer & Co were active toy makers from around 1906 through to the early 1930s. Trademarks bearing the ubiquitous fish motif (and possibly a figure in armour) are to be found on most of their production.
42, 49, 61, 67-69, 74, 76, 101, 109, 111, 118-19

GREPPERT & KELCH

G & K or Gundka were the trademarks of this company, whose production resembled Lehmann reaching the peak of their activity in the 1920s.
76-77, 100, 109

GUNTHERMANN

This notable firm was founded by S Gunthermann in 1877, and produced its first car in 1898. The company continued until 1965 when it was taken over by Siemens. Logos were based on the initials 'SG' and during the period 1903 to 1920 were combined with 'AW'.

16-18, 21, 32-33, 36-37, 41, 43, 48-49, 62, 64-65, 82-83, 86-87, 112, 118, 151

HESS

Founded at Nuremberg in 1826. The founder's son, Johann Leonhart Hess, took over the firm in 1866. A unique feature of Hessmobil cars was the friction engine. Production finished in 1934.
21, 23, 40-41, 64, 66, 84-85, 94-95, 121, 148

JEP

Founded as SIF (Société Industrielle de Ferblanterie) in 1899, the firm changed its name to J d P (Jouets de Paris) in 1928 and then to JEP (Jouets en Paris) in 1932. Jep cars generally carried the trademark of the vehicle they imitated on the radiator. The company ceased production in 1965. This firm is particularly renowned for a series of 'badge engineered' cars bearing the illustrious names Renault, Delage,

Panhard Levassor and Voisin, all on similar body pressings. In addition a Rolls Royce and a Hispano Suiza put Jep in the forefront of semi-scale toy cars. *Not illustrated*

KELLERMAN

C G Kellerman & Co of Nuremburg were a prolific maker of tin toys over a wide spectrum during the 1920s and 1930s. Their CKO trademark was seen on post war tin toys right through to the late 1970s, in particular a range of small scale cars and trucks and buses.
145

KOHNSTAM, MOSES

The firm of Moses Kohnstam was founded in Fürth during the last quarter of the nineteenth century. Its principal activity was as an agent and distributor for the small (and in many cases unknown) makers who proliferated in Southern Germany. Many of these toys bore the 'Moko' trade mark. After the Second World War, J. Kohnstam set up

in the UK and was involved as the sole distributor of Lesney products (Matchbox Toys, etc) and later the founder's grandson Richard Kohnstam marketed toy and model products under the 'Riko' trademark.
110, 126

LEHMANN

Founded by Ernst Paul Lehmann at Brandenburg in 1881. On his death in 1934 the company continued under the ownership of Johannes Richter. The Lehmann name continues today. Lehmann's name is synonymous with some of the most ingenious novelty toys from the turn of the century right through to 1939. Lehmann's name is synonymous with some of the most ingenious novelty toys from the turn of the century right through to 1939. In addition their toy vehicles were of outstanding quality.
24-27, 29, 76-79, 81, 90, 98-100, 102-08, 129-31, 133, 138, 141, 165

LEVY, GEORG

A prolific maker of cheap tin toys from the 1920s through to 1934. The company re-formed as Nuremburg Tin Toys Factory in England ceasing business in 1971.
145, 167

MARKLIN

This major toy manufacturer, founded at Goppingen in 1840, remains in business today. Cars are relatively rare as the company traditionally concentrated on the manufacture of railways with every kind of accessory, and other toys of outstanding quality such as boats.
58, 116-17, 153

METALGRAF

Founded at Milan in 1910, Metalgraf went out of business in the 1930s.
116

MINERVA

This series of British-made tin toys is thought to have been the trade mark of Cooper Bond Ltd who operated from the Minerva Works in London from 1916-1928. However the wheels of some buses from this series bear the inscription 'Smith & Kovell' who while hardly a real life tyre maker may have been a sub-contractor or successor to this line.
140 141

OROBR

This was the trademark of 'Oro' Werke Neil, Blechschmidt & Muller of Brandenburg. The firm made a series of cheap yet artistically interesting lithographed tin toys both before and after the First World War.
136

PLANK/SCHOENNER

While neither of these Nuremburg firms (founded in 1866 and 1875

respectively) were known to have produced many toy autos, both were pioneers in the field of educational and experimental toys.
20

RICHTER

This little known firm operated in Brandenburg at the turn of the century and to date cheap tin vehicles bearing the trade mark R & Co B have come to light.
50, 91

STOCK

Founded in Solingen around 1906 the company made toys with an emphasis on novelties until the 1930s. The firm's trade mark comprised two crossed walking sticks and the words 'Marke Stock'.
80

TIPP & CO

Tipp & Co, variously known as Tipco and 'TCO' (the mark always stamped on the bonnet of its cars), was founded in 1912. Tipp's owner Philip Ullmann left Germany as a political emigrant in 1933, and set up the firm of Mettoy in England. The company in Germany produced a range of military models during the war, until its factory was requisitioned for war purposes in 1942. In 1948 it resumed operations as a toy manufacturer, finally going out of business in 1971.
96, 134, 149-150, 156-62, 167-68

WELLS & CO

Wells and Co was founded in 1919 and was formed out of an earlier firm known as British Metal & Toy Manufacturers Ltd. Later Brimtoy was absorbed and during the 1930s the company was known as Wells-Brimtoy. This firm in all its guises was the largest maker of cheap tin toys in the UK and even today elements of the original firm exist as CMT Wells Kelo Ltd.
137

WK

This obscure toy maker was founded in 1895 by Wilhem Krauss in Nuremberg and in 1938 was ceded to Keim & Co.
113

Automobile

10/4155 offen

Bewegung des Verdeckes
für die offene und geschlossene Form des Automobils

10/4155 geschlossen

10/4155 **Automobil** mit Uhrwerk, polychrom lackiert mit neuer, origineller Anordnung, um den Wagen offen oder geschlossen zu haben, durch die Bewegung des Verdeckes in der durch obige Zeichnung veranschaulichten Form kann die Veränderung rasch und einfach vorgenommen werden. 24 cm lang, 10 cm breit, 9 cm hoch

Feine Automobile

10/4121/0

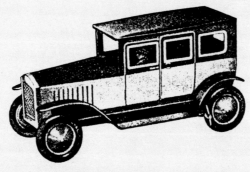

10/4121/1 mit Türen zum Öffnen

10/4151 mit 2 elektr. Scheinwerfern

10/4121/0 **Automobil**, fein polychrom lackiert, mit Spiralfeder=Aufzug . . . . 16 cm lang, 9,5 cm hoch, 7,5 cm breit

10/4121/1 **Automobil**, „ „ „ „ „ mit Türen zum Öffnen, 21 „ „ 12 „ „ 10 „ „

10/4151 **Automobil**, „ „ „ mit Uhrwerk und elektrischer Beleuchtung mit 2 Stirnlampen (Scheinwerfern) für Taschenlampenbatterie, mit Nickelkühler, Bremse, vernickelten Scheibenrädern mit Gummireifen, Windschutz, vernickelten Laternen, Reserve-Gummirad mit Schraubenschlüssel im Werkzeugkasten, 27 cm lang, 13 cm hoch, 10,5 cm breit

BIBLIOGRAPHY

'American clockwork toys 1862-1900' (Schiffer, USA, 1981)

'The art of the tin toy' (New Cavendish Books, UK, 1976)

'Attelages, automobiles et cycles' (Edita, Switzerland, 1983)

'Autohobby' (Priuli & Verlucca, Ivrea, Italy, *undated*)

'Building and collecting model automobiles' (Crown Publishers, USA, *undated*)

'Gamage's Christmas bazaar 1913' (David & Charles, UK, *undated*)

'The golden age of toys' (Edita, Switzerland, 1967)

'Lehmann toys: the history of E P Lehmann 1881-1981' (New Cavendish Books, UK, 1982)

'Mr Gamage's great toy bazaar 1902-1906' (Denys Ingram, UK, 1982)

'Model cars of the world' (Edita, Switzerland, 1967)

'Toys, dolls, games: Paris 1903-1914' (Denys Ingram, UK, 1981)

The various reprinted manufacturers' catalogues, such as those of Bing, Märklin, Carette and others from various publishers, are also recommended including the Series: Die Anderen Nürnberger (Hobby Haas, 1974).

Die von verschiedenen Verlagen herausgebrachten diversen Nachdrucke von Herstellerkatalogen wie die von Bing, Märklin, Carette u.a. können ebenfalls empfohlen werden, darunter auch die Reihe ‚Die anderen Nürnberger' (Hobby Haas, 1974).

Les nouveaux tirages de catalogues de fabricants tels que Bing, Märklin, Carette et autres catalogues publiés par divers editeurs sont également recommandés, y compris la série: Die Anderen Nürnberger (Hobby Haas 1974).

VOR 1900

Die ersten Blechspielzeugautos haben ihre Wurzeln in der Welt der zweirädrigen Droschken mit und ohne Pferde ebenso wie in der Welt des modernen Kraftfahrzeugs.

Da sie sich so wenig auf reale Vorbilder stützten, dank der phantasievollen Verwendung von Farben und durch die Erfindergabe, die sich in öffnenden Türen, drehenden Rädern und anderen funktionsfähigen Details manifestierte, erreichten diese frühen Blechspielzeugautos ein Ausmaß an schöpferischer Phantasie und Freiheit, das man bei modernen Spielzeugen oft vergeblich sucht.

AVANT 1900

Les premières petites voitures en fer blanc tenaient autant du fiacre et de la voiture "sans chevaux" que de l'automobile moderne. Grâce à la finesse évidente de leur base, à l'imagination fertile dont les fabricants faisaient preuve dans le choix des couleurs, et aux mécanismes ingénieux permettant d'ouvrir les portes, de faire tourner les roues, et d'autres détails de fonctionnement, les premières petites voitures ont atteint un niveau de création et d'invention que l'on trouve moins fréquemment dans les jouets modernes.

BEFORE 1900

The first tin toy cars belonged as much to the world of hansom cabs and horseless carriages as to that of the modern motor car.

Because of their slender basis in reality, their makers' imaginative use of colour, and the ingenuity displayed in creating doors that opened, wheels that turned and other working details, the early toy autos achieved a fantasy and freedom less easily found in modern toys.

a GÜNTHERMANN Horseless carriage, 16cm (6.3in). One of the earliest Günthermann cars, probably dating from c1895. It features adjustable steering, unusually good embossing, and lithography of fine quality. The original driver is missing.

a GÜNTHERMANN Motorkutsche, 16cm. Dieses wahrscheinlich um 1895 hergestellte Auto ist eines der frühesten Günthermann-Modelle. Charakteristisch sind die verstellbare Lenkung, eine ungewöhnlich gute Prägung und eine hohe Druckqualität. Der originale Fahrer fehlt.

a GÜNTHERMANN Voiture sans chevaux, 16cm. C'est l'une des premières voitures Günthermann, elle date probablement d'environ 1895. Elle se caractérise par sa direction réglable, un estampage particulièrement bien fait, et une gravure de belle qualité. Le conducteur d'origine manque.

a

b BING Spider, 32cm (12.6in). A rare Bing Spider with real leather seats and rubber tyres. The version with steam-operated motor is better known. The driver is not original.

b BING Spider, 32cm. Ein seltener Spider von Bing mit echten Ledersitzen und Gummireifen. Bekannter ist die Ausführung mit Dampfmaschinenantrieb. Der Fahrer gehört nicht zur Originalausstattung.

b BING Spider, 32cm. Rare voiture Bing spider avec sièges en cuir véritable et pneus en caoutchouc. On connaît davantage la version comprenant un moteur à vapeur. Le conducteur n'est pas d'origine.

c GÜNTHERMANN Vis-à-vis, 29cm (11.4in). This is the largest Günthermann vis-à-vis, and features lithographed bodywork, adjustable steering, and rubber tyres. It is based on a contemporary Peugeot motor car. The handpainted driver is original.

c GÜNTHERMANN Vis-à-vis, 29cm. Dies ist der größte Vis-à-vis Günthermanns. Der Aufbau ist bedruckt, die Lenkung ist verstellbar und die Räder haben Gummireifen. Die Vorlage war ein zeitgenössischer Peugeot. Der handbemalte Fahrer ist original.

c GÜNTHERMANN Vis-à-vis, 29cm. C'est le plus grand vis-à-vis existant, de Günthermann, la carrosserie est représentée en lithographie, la direction est réglable, et les pneus sont en caoutchouc. Il s'inspire d'une voiture Peugeot contemporaine, le conducteur peint à la main, est d'origine.

b

c

a GÜNTHERMANN Single-seater, 14cm (5.5in). A single-seater clockwork racing car, with 'Paris-Berlin' lithographed onto the top of the bonnet, suggesting that this toy was made to catch the enthusiasm generated by the early Gordon Bennet road races.

a GÜNTHERMANN Einsitzer, 14cm. Ein einsitziger Rennwagen mit Feder-werkantrieb und dem Aufdruck „Paris-Berlin" auf der Haube. Es ist möglich, daß dieser Wagen geschaffen wurde, um die Begeisterung für die ersten Straßenrennen von Gordon Bennet auszunutzen.

a GÜNTHERMANN Voiture à une place, 14cm. Voiture de course mécanique à une place portant "Paris-Berlin" lithographié sur le haut du capot. Ce qui laisse penser que ce jouet fut fait pour capter l'enthousiasme que suscitèrent les premières courses sur route de Gordon Bennet.

b GÜNTHERMANN Vis-à-vis, 12.5cm (4.9in). Lithographed bodywork, rubber tyres, and handpainted figure; c1905.

b GÜNTHERMANN Vis-à-vis, 12,5cm. Bedruckter Aufbau, Gummiräder und eine handbemalte Figur; um 1905.

b GÜNTHERMANN Vis-à-vis, 12,5cm. Carrosserie lithographiée, pneus en caoutchouc et figurine peinte à la main. Vers 1905.

c GÜNTHERMANN Horseless carriage, 22cm (8.7in). The wheels have rubber tyres, and the vehicle can be steered. Fine lithography effectively simulates seat upholstery. Two rear figures are missing, and the driver is not original. c1904.

c GÜNTHERMANN Motorkutsche, 22cm. Die Räder haben Gummiberei-fungen, und das Fahrzeug ist lenkbar. Die Polster werden gut durch den hochwertigen Druck imitiert. Zwei Figuren fehlen, und auch der Fahrer gehört nicht zur Originalausstattung. Ca. 1904.

c GÜNTHERMANN Voiture sans chevaux 22cm. Ses roues ont des pneus en caoutchouc, et le véhicule peut être dirigé. Une lithographie de qualité simule de façon réaliste le capitonnage des sièges. Deux figurines manquent à l'arrière, et le conducteur n'est pas d'origine. Vers 1904.

a

b

c

d Maker unknown Vis-à-vis, 11.5cm
(4.5in). Possibly by Carette, and
probably marketed by Moses
Kohnstam. A simple but brightly
lithographed vis-à-vis, constructed in
the same manner as penny toys but
slightly larger and fitted with a small
clockwork motor. The steering is
incorporated in the mechanism.

d Hersteller unbekannt Vis-à-vis,
11,5cm. Möglicherweise von Carette
hergestellt und wahrscheinlich von
Moses Kohnstam verkauft. Ein
einfacher, hell bedruckter Vis-à-vis
in ähnlicher Bauweise wie Pfennig-
spielzeug, doch etwas größer und mit
einem kleinen Federwerkantrieb
ausgerüstet. Die Lenkung ist im
Antriebsmechanismus untergebracht.

d Fabricant inconnu Vis-à-vis, 11,5cm.
Il est possible qu'il ait été fabriqué
par Carette et commercialisé par
Moses Kohnstam. C'est un vis-à-vis
simple mais lithographié dans des
couleurs vives. Construit de la même
manière que les jouets à deux sous
il est légèrement plus grand et muni
d'un petit moteur mécanique.
La direction est incorporée au
mécanisme.

d

e German maker, unknown Vis-à-vis,
16.5cm (6.5in). Possibly by Carette,
this is a larger and slightly more
elaborate vis-à-vis, with white rubber
tyres and a clockwork mechanism. It
may have been marketed by Moses
Kohnstam.

e Deutschland, Hersteller unbekannt
Vis-à-vis, 16,5cm. Dieser wahrscheinlich von Carette stammende Vis-à-vis
ist größer und etwas verfeinerter.
Er hat weiße Gummiräder und einen
Federwerkantrieb. Er wurde
möglicherweise von Moses Kohnstam
vertrieben.

e Fabricant allemand inconnu
Vis-à-vis, 16,5cm. Peut être de
Carette, ce vis-à-vis est plus grand et
légèrement plus élaboré que le
précédent, avec ses pneus en
caoutchouc blanc et son dispositif
mécanique. Il se peut qu'il ait été
commercialisé par Moses Kohnstam.

e

German, possibly PLANK or SCHOENNER Steam-driven tricycle, 20cm (7.9in). One of the earliest self-propelled toy vehicles. The flywheel is driven by an oscillating motor powered by a vertical steam boiler, with a single cast cylinder. This drives the two rear wheels. The rudimentary body consists of bent wire. Originally a small plaster figure was sold with this vehicle.

Deutschland, vielleicht PLANK oder SCHOENNER Dampfbetriebenes Dreiradfahrzeug, 20cm. Eines der ältesten Spielzeugfahrzeuge mit Eigenantrieb. Der Schwungradantrieb erfolgt über einen pulsierenden Motor von einer vertikalen Dampfmaschine mit einem Gußzylinder und wirkt auf die Hinterräder. Die Karosserie wird durch Drahtbügel angedeutet. Mit dem Fahrzeug wurde eine kleine Gipsfigur verkauft.

Tricycle à vapeur allemand probablement PLANK ou SCHOENNER, 20cm. C'est l'un des premiers jouets auto-moteur. Le volant de commande est entrainé par un moteur oscillant actionné par une chaudière à vapeur verticale d'un seul cylindre moulé. Ceci entraine les deux roues arrière. La carosserie rudimentaire est faite de fil de fer courbé. A l'origine, une petite figurine de plâtre etait vendue avec ce véhicule.

GÜNTHERMANN Horseless
carriages, 17cm, 12cm and 11cm
(6.7in, 4.7in, and 4.3in). A group of
three clockwork Günthermann
horseless carriages made in the late
1890s through to c1910. The vehicle
on the left with white rubber tyres is
probably the earliest of the group.

GÜNTHERMANN Motordroschken,
17cm, 12cm und 11cm. Drei von
Günthermann ab Ende der neunziger
Jahre bis etwa 1910 hergestellte
Motordroschken mit Federwerkantrieb. Das Fahrzeug links mit den
weißen Gummireifen ist wahrscheinlich das älteste der Gruppe.

GÜNTHERMANN Coupés 17cm,
12cm, et 11cm. Groupe de trois
coupés mécaniques, fabriqués par
Günthermann à la fin des années
1890 jusqu'en 1910 environ. Le
véhicule à pneus de caoutchouc
reproduit à gauche est probablement
le plus ancien du groupe.

HESS Open two-seater, 22.6cm
(8.9in). A rare and early Hess
flywheel-driven lithographed car,
evocative of the heroic early road
racing cars.

HESS offener Zweisitzer, 22,6cm.
Ein seltenes und frühes bedrucktes
Auto von Hess mit Schwungrad-
antrieb. Es erinnert an die heroische
Zeit der ersten Rennwagen.

HESS Voiture deux places, ouverte,
22,6cm. Rare et ancienne voiture
Hess lithographiée, entraînée par son
volant à synergie elle évoque les
temps héroïques des pionniers des
courses sur route.

Maker unknown Horseless carriage, 16cm (6.3in). The maker of this early toy is probably French, c1893. The porcelain headed driver wears cloth garments.

Hersteller unbekannt Motorkutsche, 16cm. Dieses frühe Spielzeug wurde wahrscheinlich um 1893 in Frankreich hergestellt. Der Fahrer hat einen Porzellankopf und trägt Stoffkleidung.

Fabricant inconnu. Voiture sans chevaux, 16cm. Le fabricant de cet ancien jouet est probablement français, vers 1893. Le conducteur habillé de tissu a une tête de porcelaine.

HESS Horseless carriage, c1898 22cm (8.7in). This unusual car is one of the earliest by this manufacturer. It has no steering but features a flywheel mechanism so favoured by Hess, in place of a clockwork motor that would have been used by most other German makers. Note the heavily embossed simulated-leather seats.

HESS Motorkutsche, 22cm. Dieser ungewöhnliche Wagen ist einer der ältesten dieses Herstellers. Er hat keine Lenkung, aber anstelle des von den meisten anderen deutschen Herstellern verwendeten Federwerks den von Hess bevorzugten Schwungradantrieb. Man beachte die stark geprägte Ledersitzimitation.

HESS Voiture sans chevaux, (vers 1898) 22cm. Cette voiture inhabituelle est une des premières construites par ce fabricant. Elle n'a pas de direction mais contient le mécanisme à volant préféré par Hess au lieu du moteur mécanique adopté par la plupart des autres fabricants allemands. Notez les sièges fortement estampés simulant le cuir.

LEHMANN 'Li La' (EPL 520), 14cm (5.5in). A multi-action novelty based on the London hansom cab, here transformed into a horseless carriage. As the vehicle moves along, the two ladies beat the dog in a vain attempt to drive it away from the carriage. It is one of Lehmann's most amusing and intricate novelty toys. The vehicle is lithographed and the figures handpainted.

LEHMANN „Li La" (EPL 520), 14cm. Eine auf der Londoner Pferdedroschke basierende Trickneuheit, hier als Motordroschke ausgeführt. Während der Fahrt schlagen die beiden Damen auf den Hund ein, um ihn von der Droschke zu vertreiben. Eine der amüsantesten und kompliziertesten Neuheiten Lehmanns. Das Fahrzeug ist bedruckt, die Figuren sind handbemalt.

LEHMANN "Li La" (EPL 520), 14cm. Une nouveauté à mécanismes multiples inspirée du cab de Londres transformé ici en coupé. Au fur et à mesure que le véhicule avance, les deux dames battent le chien pour essayer vainement de l'éloigner du véhicule. C'est l'un des jouets le plus amusant et le plus compliqué de Lehmann. Le véhicule est lithographié et les figurines peintes à la main.

LEHMANN 'Baker and chimney sweep' (EPL 450), 12cm (4.7in). This amusing novelty toy has a typical Lehmann action. The baker rides his tricycle while at the same time attempting to beat off the sweep who is attacking him from the rear with his broom. The cake on the cart is actually a bell which rings as the toy moves.

LEHMANN „Bäcker und Schornstein-feger" (EPL 450), 12cm. Diese humorvolle Neuheit ist ein typisches Lehmann-Spielzeug: während der Bäcker sein Dreirad fährt, wehrt er gleichzeitig den Schornsteinfeger ab, der ihn von hinten mit seinem Besen angreift. Der Kuchen auf dem Wagen ist in Wirklichkeit eine Glocke, die während der Fahrt klingelt.

LEHMANN "Boulanger et ramoneur" (EPL 450), 12cm. Cette amusante nouveauté a un mécanicien Lehmann typique. Le boulanger, tout en conduisant son tricycle, essaie de taper sur le ramoneur qui l'attaque par derrière avec son balai. Le gâteau posé sur la charrette est en fait une cloche qui tinte quand le jouet bouge.

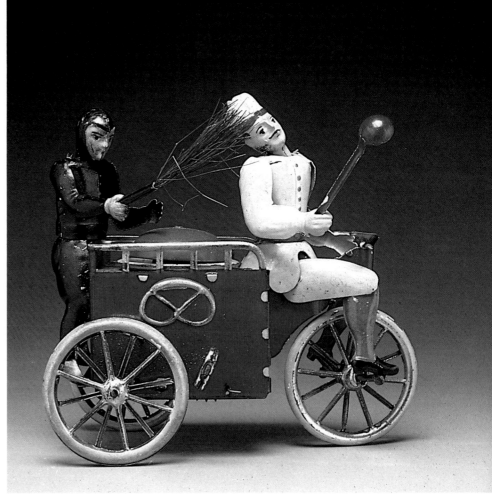

LEHMANN 'Naughty boy' (EPL 495), 11.5cm (4.6in). A small clockwork vis-à-vis, with an erratic movement produced by the actions of the sailorsuited boy from whom the car's name is derived. The main car is lithographed and the first two figures handpainted.

LEHMANN „Ungezogener Junge" (EPL 495), 11,5cm. Ein kleiner Feder-werk-Vis-à-vis. Seine ruckweise Fahrt ergibt sich durch die Bewegungen des Jungen (daher der Name des Wagens) im Matrosenanzug. Der Aufbau ist bedruckt, die beiden Figuren sind handbemalt.

LEHMANN "Vilain Garçon" (EPL 495), 11,5cm. Petit vis-à-vis mécanique, au mouvement irrégulier produit par le mécanisme du garçon en costume de marin qui donne son nom au jouet. Le corps de la voiture est lithographié et les deux figurines sont peintes à la main.

LEHMANN 'Am Pol' (EPL 681), 16cm (6.3in). An early tricycle road vehicle made in two versions. The one illustrated commemorates Amundsen's polar exploration, which is why the umbrella represents the globe and the figures appear to be dressed in furs. As the vehicle moves along, the umbrella turns and the driver moves his right hand up and down. It continued in production from c1905 to c1914.

LEHMANN „Am Pol" (EPL 681), 16cm. Ein frühes, in zwei Versionen hergestelltes Dreiradfahrzeug. Das in der Abbildung erinnerte an die Polarexpedition Amundsens, da der Schirm die Gestalt eines Globus hat und die Figuren offenbar in Pelze gekleidet sind. Während der Fahrt dreht sich der Schirm, und die rechte Hand des Fahrers bewegt sich auf

und ab. Das Spielzeug wurde von ca. 1905 bis ca. 1914 hergestellt.

LEHMANN "Am Pol" (EPL 681), 16cm. Un des premiers tricycles allant sur route il fut fabriqué en deux versions. Celle qui est reproduite ici commémore l'exploration solaire d'Amundson, ce qui explique que le parapluie soit orné du globe terrestre et que les figurines soient habillées de fourrures. Quant le véhicule avance, le parapluie tourne et le conducteur lève et baisse le bras. Il resta en fabrication de 1905 à 1914 environ.

LEHMANN 'Also' Open two-seater (EPL 700), 10.5cm (4.1in). A typical small Lehmann car bearing a characteristically whimsical name. It continued in production during the 1920s and 1930s.

LEHMANN „Also" (EPL 700), (offener Zweisitzer), 10,5cm. Ein typischer kleiner Lehmann-Wagen mit einem ausgefallenen Namen. Er wurde in den zwanziger und dreißiger Jahren hergestellt.

LEHMANN "Also" (EPL 700), voiture deux places ouverte, 10,5cm. C'est un petit jouet typique de Lehmann qui porte un nom fantaisiste significant: "Aussi". Il fut fabriqué jusque dans les années 1920-1930.

LEHMANN 'Oho' (EPL 545), 22cm (8.5in). Ernst Paul Lehmann was a member of a humorous society whose members used various catchphrases when drinking toasts. Lehmann registered some of these as names for his toys. 'Oho' was a toast used after club debates. The vehicle has adjustable steering.

LEHMANN „Oho" (EPL 545), 22cm. Ernst Paul Lehmann war Mitglied eines Geselligkeitsvereins, in dem verschiedene Schlagworte bei Trinksprüchen benutzt wurden. Lehmann ließ einige davon als Namen für seine Spielzeuge eintragen. „Oho" wurde als Trinkspruch nach Klubdebatten benutzt.

LEHMANN "Oho" (EPL 545), 22cm. Ernst Paul Lehmann faisait partie d'une coterie pleine d'esprit dont les membres employaient diverses expressions clef en portant des toasts. Lehmann en déposa certaines dont il baptisa ses jouets. "Oho" accompagnait le toast qu'on portait après les débats du club. Ce véhicule a une direction réglable.

German, maker unknown Three-wheeler, 13cm (5.1in). The manufacturer of this lithographed three-wheeler is unknown.

Deutschland, Hersteller unbekannt Dreiradfahrzeug, 13cm. Der Hersteller dieses bedruckten Dreiradfahrzeugs ist nicht bekannt.

Fabricant allemand. Tricycle 13cm. Jouet lithographié.

French, maker unknown Tricycle, 12cm (4.7in). A handpainted clockwork tricycle with lead wheels.

Frankreich, Hersteller unbekannt Dreirad, 12cm. Ein handbemaltes Aufzieh-Dreirad mit Bleirädern.

Fabricant français inconnu. Tricycle 12cm. Tricycle mécanique peint à la main et muni de roues en plomb.

LEHMANN 'Motorkutsche' (EPL 420), 13cm (5.1in). Electric coaches were used in England and Europe for local transport. This early Lehmann automobile is powered by a coil-spring motor, and features an ingenious pre-adjustable steering mechanism. The stylish driver is original, the bystanders are contemporary.

LEHMANN Motorkutsche (EPL 420), 13cm. Für den städtischen Transport wurden in England und auf dem Kontinent Elektrobusse benutzt. Dieses frühe Fahrzeug von Lehmann hat einen Spiralfederaufzug und einen Lenkmechanismus. Der Fahrer ist original; die beiden Figuren sind Bleifiguren aus der Zeit.

LEHMANN Landaulet électrique (EPL 420), 13cm. En Europe et en Angleterre on utilisait des véhicules électriques pour les transports locaux. Cette voiture Lehmann, l'une des toutes premières, est actionnée par un moteur à ressort en spirale et possède un ingénieux mécanisme de direction pré-réglable. L'élégant conducteur est d'origine, tandis que les spectateurs sont contemporains.

1900-1914

In dem Maße, wie sich der Kraftwagen weiterentwickelte und durchsetzte, spiegelten auch die Spielzeugautos die schnell aufeinanderfolgenden Entwicklungen und Neuerungen der echten Vorbilder wider. Die technischen Fortschritte des echten Kraftwagens führten zu mechanischen Neuerungen auch bei ihren Spielzeuggegenstücken.

Die führenden Spielzeughersteller entwickelten neue Verfahren der Blechbearbeitung und der Drucktechnik, mit denen es ihnen möglich wurde, den Geist des Kraftfahrzeugs der Vorkriegsjahre einzufangen. Die frühen Rennwagen, die offenen Tourenwagen und die Limousinen wurden alle farbenfroh und mit Begeisterung zur Sache interpretiert.

1900-1914

Au fur et à mesure du développement et de l'utilisation de l'automobile, les petites voitures se sont mises à refléter l'évolution rapide et les innovations des vraies voitures. Les progrès technologiques réalisés dans la construction automobile ont inspiré l'esprit d'invention qui a marqué les qualités mécaniques de leurs modèles réduits.

Les grands fabricants de jouets mirent au point des techniques de moulage et des procédés lithographiques qui leur permirent de saisir l'esprit qui animait la construction automobile dans la période d'avant-guerre. Les premiers modèles de voiture de course, les torpédos, les conduites intérieures, étaient tous interprétés dans des couleurs chatoyantes avec grand enthousiasme.

1900-1914

As the motor car developed and established itself, toy cars reflected the fast-moving developments and innovations of real cars. The technological advances in real cars prompted mechanical inventiveness in their toy counterparts.

The great toymakers developed techniques of tin pressing and lithography which enabled them to catch the spirit of prewar motoring. The early racing cars, open touring cars, and saloons were all interpreted colourfully and enthusiastically.

GÜNTHERMANN Open four-seater, 19cm (7.5in). All four figures are original. The car features rubber tyres and adjustable steering.

GÜNTHERMANN Offener Viersitzer, 19cm. Die vier Figuren gehören zur Originalausstattung. Der Wagen hat Gummireifen und eine verstellbare Lenkung.

GÜNTHERMANN Voiturette quatre-places ouverte, 19cm. Les quatre figurines sont d'origine. La voiture se caractérise par des pneus en caout-chouc et une direction réglable.

CARETTE Rear-entrance tonneau, 31cm (12.2in). This lithographed open tonneau features cast wheels with white rubber tyres and originally handpainted figures. One lady passenger at the rear is missing.

CARETTE Offener Wagen mit Rückeinstieg, 31cm. Dieser bedruckte offene Wagen mit Rückeinstieg hat Gußräder mit weißen Gummireifen und ursprünglich handbemalte Figuren. Auf dem Rücksitz fehlt eine Dame.

CARETTE Tonneau muni d'une entrée arrière, 31cm. Ce tonneau ouvert se caractérise par des roues moulées avec des pneus en caoutchouc blanc et des figurines d'origine peintes à la main. Il manque une passagère à l'arrière.

Maker unknown Open four-seater,
14.5cm (5.7in). This lithographed car
has adjustable steering and is
German-made.

Hersteller unbekannt Offener
Viersitzer, 14,5cm. Dieser bedruckte
Wagen hat eine verstellbare Lenkung
und wurde in Deutschland hergestellt.

Fabricant inconnu. Voiture quatre-
places ouverte, 14,5cm. Cette voiture
lithographiée a une direction
réglable. Elle est de fabrication
allemande.

Maker unknown Two-seat open
tourer, 23cm (9.1in). Handpainted,
with adjustable steering, rubber
wheels, and a clockwork mechanism.
German made, possibly by Karl Bub.

Hersteller unbekannt Zweisitziger
offener Tourenwagen, 23cm. Der
handbemalte Wagen mit verstellbarer
Lenkung, Gummirädern und
Federwerk stammt aus Deutschland,
wahrscheinlich von Karl Bub.

Fabricant inconnu. Voiturette deux-
places, 23cm. Voiture peinte à la
main, à direction réglable, roues de
caoutchouc et mouvement mécanique,
elle fut fabriquée en Allemagne, peut-
être par Karl Bub.

Maker unknown Open tourer, 20.5cm (7.9in). This finely lithographed tourer features adjustable steering, simple disc wheels, and interesting lithographed lady passengers in the rear.

Hersteller unbekannt Offener Tourenwagen, 20,5cm. Dieser hübsch bedruckte Tourenwagen hat eine verstellbare Lenkung, einfache Scheibenräder und auffällig bedruckte Damen im Fond.

fabricant inconnu. Double phaéton, 20,5cm. Cette voiture, joliment lithographiée, est caractérisée par sa direction réglable, de simples disques formant les roues et d'intéressantes passagères lithographiées à l'arrière.

c GÜNTHERMANN Landaulette, 20.5cm (7.9in). A bright and busy small Landaulette. It features a folding leather roof, glass windscreen, opening rear doors, adjustable steering, large headlights and a handpainted chauffeur.

c GÜNTHERMANN Landaulet, 20,5cm. Ein heller und schnittiger kleiner Halblandauer mit faltbarem Lederverdeck, Glaswindschutz-scheibe, sich öffnenden hinteren Türen, verstellbarer Lenkung, großen Scheinwerfern und einem handbemalten Chauffeur.

c GÜNTHERMANN Landaulet, 20,5cm. Petit landaulet clair et plein d'allant. Il se caractérise par un pare-brise de verre, un toit ouvrant en cuir, des portes arrière qui s'ouvrent, une direction réglable; de grands phares et un chauffeur peint à la main.

c

b

a

a Maker unknown Saloon, 24cm (9.5in). Possibly by Karl Bub. Rubber tyres are a feature of this saloon.

a Hersteller unbekannt, möglicher-weise von Karl Bub. Limousine, 24cm. Diese Limousine ist mit Gummi-bereifung ausgerüstet.

a Fabricant inconnu. Limousine, 24cm. Probablement fabriquée par Karl Bub. Cette limousine intérieure est munie de pneus en caoutchouc.

b BING Town coupé, 22cm (8.7in). A small high-quality handpainted town car featuring white rubber tyres, nickel-plated headlights, brass louvres on the bonnet, and opening rear doors.

b BING Coupé, 22cm. Ein kleines, hochwertiges hand-bemaltes Coupé für den Stadtverkehr mit Gummireifen, vernickelten Scheinwerfern, Messinglamellen an der Motorhaube und sich öffnenden Hintertüren.

b BING Coupé de ville, 22cm. Petite voiture de ville de grande qualité, peinte à la main, caractérisée par des pneus en caoutchouc blanc, des phares recouverts de nickel, des auvents de capot en cuivre et des portes arrière qui s'ouvrent.

Maker unknown High-roofed rear-entrance tonneau, 24cm (9.4in). The quality of lithography on this car is extremely high, reminiscent of that of Carette and Günthermann. However, neither the mechanism nor the metal pressings are found on any car known to be made by them, which suggests that the maker is another German manufacturer – possibly Karl Bub. The four figures are tin.

CARETTE Two examples of 'No.50', both 22cm (8.7in). Open and closed versions of this toy, both with rubber wheels, fine gold and red lithography, and lively handpainted figures.

CARETTE Zwei Muster des „Nr. 50", beide 22cm. Eine offene und eine geschlossene Ausführung dieses Spielzeugs. Beide haben Gummiräder, sind sorgfältig goldfarben und rot bedruckt und haben hübsche handbemalte Figuren.

CARETTE Deux modèles N°. 50, 22cm chacun. Versions ouverte et fermée de ce jouet, qui ont toutes deux des pneus en caoutchouc, une belle lithographie rouge et or, et des figurines peintes à la main de façon vivante.

Hersteller unbekannt Rückeinstieg-wagen mit hohem Dach, 24cm. Die Druckqualität dieses Wagens ist ungewöhnlich gut und erinnert an Carette und Günthermann. Da jedoch weder der Mechanismus, noch die Metallprägeteile an Wagen dieser beiden Firmen verwendet wurden, muß auf einen anderen deutschen Hersteller geschlossen werden, möglicherweise Karl Bub.

Fabricant inconnu. Tonneau à toit surélevé et à entrée arrière, 24cm. La très belle qualité de lithographie de cette voiture fait penser à Carette et Günthermann. Cependant, les voitures fabriquées par ces derniers n'emploient ni ce mécanisme ni cette façon d'emboutir le métal, ce qui donne à penser qu'il s'agirait d'un autre fabricant allemand. Peut-être Karl Bub. Les quatre figurines sont en étain.

Maker unknown Landaulette taxi,
25cm (9.8in). This variant of the car
illustrated on the left has a taxi meter
and adjustable steering. Again,
possibly made by Karl Bub.

Hersteller unbekannt Taxi-Landaulet,
25cm. Diese Abwandlung des links
abgebildeten Wagens hat einen
Taxameter und eine verstellbare
Lenkung. Möglicherweise ebenfalls
von Karl Bub.

Maker unknown Two-seater, 24cm
(9.4in). A further variant of the two
cars on the left. Possibly by Karl Bub.

Hersteller unbekannt Zweisitzer,
24cm. Eine weitere Abwandlung der
beiden links abgebildeten Wagen.
Möglicherweise von Karl Bub.

Fabricant inconnu. Taxi-landaulet,
25cm. Cette variante de la voiture
reproduite à gauche a un compteur
de taxi et une direction réglable.
Peut-être Karl Bub.

Fabricant inconnu. Voiturette deux-
places, 24cm. Autre variante des
deux voitures de gauche. Peut-être
Karl Bub.

handpainted driver.

b GÜNTHERMANN Viertürige Limousine, 30cm. Dieses bedruckte Auto hat vier sich öffnende Türen, einen Dachgepäckträger und einen handbemalten Fahrer.

b GÜNTHERMANN Limousine à quatre portes, 30cm. Cette voiture lithographiée se caractérise par quatre portes ouvrantes, une galerie sur le toit et un conducteur peint à la main.

b

a HESS Saloon, 26cm (10.2in).
A very well lithographed and pressed tin Limousine by Hess, featuring the typical flywheel mechanism, two opening doors, and glass windows. Even the insides of the doors feature delightful lithography.

a HESS Limousine, 26cm.
Eine in hoher Güte bedruckte und gestanzte Blechspielzeuglimousine von Hess mit dem charakteristischen Schwungradmechanismus, zwei sich öffnenden Türen und Glasfenstern. Selbst die Innenseiten der Türen sind geschmackvoll bedruckt.

a HESS Limousine, 26cm.
Limousine en tôle de Hess, le laminage et la lithographie sont de belle qualité. Son mécanisme à volant est typique. Ses deux portes s'ouvrent.

c EBERL Saloon, 38cm (15in).
Two opening doors, a brake lever and adjustable steering are features of this car.

c EBERL Limousine, 38cm.
Zwei sich öffnende Türen, ein Bremshebel und eine verstellbare Lenkung sind die Merkmale dieses Wagens.

c EBERL Limousine, 38cm.
Les deux portes s'ouvrent un levier de frein et une direction réglable caractérisent cette voiture.

FISCHER Open four-seat tourer, 34cm
(13.4in). A stylish open four-seat
tourer featuring electric headlights,
clockwork motor, and adjustable
steering. The plaster driver is not
original.

FISCHER Offener viersitziger
Tourenwagen, 34cm. Ein eleganter
offener viersitziger Tourenwagen mit
elektrischen Scheinwerfern,
Federwerkantrieb und verstellbarer
Lenkung. Der aus Gips hergestellte
Fahrer ist nicht original.

FISCHER Double phaéton 34cm.
Elégante voiture quatre-places,
caractérisée par des phares
électriques, un moteur mécanique et
une direction réglable. Le conducteur
de plâtre n'est pas d'origine.

BUB Open four-seat tourer, 32cm
(13in). This tourer by Karl Bub
features adjustable steering.

BUB Offener viersitziger
Tourenwagen, 32cm. Dieser
Tourenwagen von Karl Bub hat eine
verstellbare Lenkung.

BUB Double phaéton, 32cm.
Cette voiture de Karl Bub est
caractérisée par sa direction
réglable.

b GÜNTHERMANN Open four-seat car, 22cm (8.5in). Adjustable steering, rubber wheels; the driver is not original.

b GÜNTHERMANN Offener Viersitzer, 22cm. Lenkbar und mit Gummirädern. Der Fahrer ist nicht original.

b GÜNTHERMANN Double phaéton, 22cm. Direction réglable, roues en caoutchouc, le conducteur n'est pas d'origine.

b

a

a CARETTE Rear-entrance tonneau, 25cm (9.8in). A c1906 tonneau featuring high-quality lithography and white rubber tyres. This car was originally sold with four composition figures.

a CARETTE Wagen mit Rückeinstieg, 25cm. Ein um etwa 1906 hergestellter Wagen mit Rückeinstieg, in hochwertiger Druckarbeit und mit weißen Gummireifen. Dieser Wagen wurde ursprünglich mit vier zusammengehörenden Figuren verkauft.

a CARETTE Tonneau à entrée arrière, 25cm. Tonneau datant d'environ 1906, caractérisé par sa lithographie de haute qualité et ses pneus en caoutchouc blanc. Cette voiture était vendue à l'origine avec quatre figurines d'accompagnement.

c

c CARETTE Open four-seat tourer, 30cm (11.8in). The folding roof is cloth. The steering is adjustable and the brake lever operable. The driver is typically Carette.

c CARETTE Offener viersitziger Tourenwagen, 30cm. Das Faltverdeck besteht aus Stoff. Die Lenkung ist verstellbar, und der Bremshebel läßt sich betätigen. Der Fahrer ist typisch für Carette.

c CARETTE Double phaéton, 30cm. Le toit décapotable est en toile. La direction est réglable et le levier de frein fonctionne. Le conducteur est caractéristique de Carette.

c BING Open four-seater, 43cm
(16.9in). The front window is of glass;
there is a luggage rack at the rear.
The doors open and the steering is
adjustable. The chauffeur is original,
but the passengers are not.

c BING Offener Viersitzer, 43cm.
Der Wagen hat eine gläserne Windschutzscheibe und einen Heckgepäckträger. Die Türen lassen sich
öffnen, und die Lenkung ist verstellbar. Der Chauffeur gehört zur Originalausstattung, die Passagiere wurden
später hinzugefügt.

c BING Voiture quatre-places
ouverte, 43cm. La vitre de devant est
en verre. Elle comporte un porte-
bagages à l'arrière. Les portes
s'ouvrent, la direction est réglable. Le
chauffeur est d'origine mais pas les
passagers.

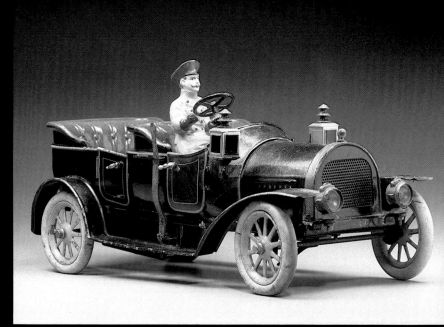

a BING Open four-seat tourer, 32cm
(12.6in). This open tourer features a
lithographed body and adjustable
steering.

a BING Offener viersitziger
Tourenwagen, 32cm. Dieser offene
Tourenwagen hat einen bedruckten
Aufbau und eine verstellbare
Lenkung.

a BING Double phaéton, 32cm.
Cette voiture a une carrosserie lithographiée et une direction réglable.

b BING Open four-seater, 33cm
(13in). This is handpainted, with
rubber tyres and an operable
steering wheel.

b BING Offener Viersitzer, 33cm.
Der Wagen ist handbemalt, hat Gummireifen und ein drehbares Lenkrad.

b BING Double phaéton, 33cm.
Ce modèle est peint à la main, muni
de pneus en caoutchouc et d'un
volant qui marche.

Maker unknown High-roofed tonneau, 21cm (8.3in). This German-made car resembles Carettes of the period. But the inferior lithography suggests a different manufacturer, as yet unidentified; possibly by Richter & Co.

Fabricant inconnu. Tonneau à toit surélevé, 21cm. Cette voiture de fabrication allemande ressemble aux voitures Carette de l'époque. Mais la mauvaise qualité de la lithographie donne à penser qu'il s'agirait d'un autre fabricant qui n'a pas encore été identifié; peut-être de Richter et Co.

BING Group of 1904 de Dion motor cars, 21cm, 25cm, and 17cm (8.3in, 9.8in and 6.7in). These all feature handpainted body work, rubber tyres, simulated button leather upholstery, and a clockwork motor. The steering is adjustable.

BING De Dion-Gruppe von 1904, 21cm, 25cm und 17cm. Alle Wagen haben handbemalte Aufbauten, Gummireifen, simulierte Lederpolster mit Polsternägeln und ein Federwerk. Die Lenkung ist verstellbar.

Hersteller unbekannt Viersitzer mit hohem Dach, 21cm. Dieser deutsche Wagen erinnert an die zeit-genössischen Carettes. Der weniger sorgfältig ausgeführte Druck läßt jedoch einen anderen Hersteller – vielleicht Richter & Co. – vermuten.

BING Groupe de Dion de 1904, 21cm, 25cm et 17cm. Tous ces modèles se caractérisent par une carrosserie peinte à la main, des pneus en caoutchouc, des boutons de cuir qui imitent le capitonnage et un moteur mécanique. La direction est réglable.

BING Open four-seat tourer, 25cm (9.8in). This c1908 tourer is handpainted with detailed embossing on the seats and white rubber tyres; it also features four opening doors and four cast metal lights, the front two of which are missing.

BING Offener viersitziger Tourenwagen, 25cm. Dieser hand-bemalte Tourenwagen von ca. 1908 hat eine detaillierte Prägung der Sitze und weiße Gummireifen. Er hat ferner vier sich öffnende Türen und ur-sprünglich vier Gußscheinwerfer, von denen die beiden vorderen fehlen.

BING Double phaéton, 25cm. Cette voiture datant d'environ 1908, est peinte à la main, l'estampage des sièges est détaillé et les pneus sont en caoutchouc blanc. Elle est aussi caractérisée par quatre portes qui s'ouvrent et quatre phares en métal moulé dont les deux de l'avant manquent.

a GÜNTHERMANN Saloon, 25cm (9.8in). This interesting Günthermann saloon features two opening doors and adjustable steering. It is modelled on an Electromobil.

a GÜNTHERMANN Limousine, 25cm. Diese interessante Limousine von Günthermann hat zwei sich öffnende Türen und eine verstellbare Lenkung. Sie ist einem Elektrofahrzeug nachgebildet.

a GÜNTHERMANN Limousine, 25cm. Cette intéressante limousine de Günthermann a deux portes qui s'ouvrent et une conduite réglable. Elle est conçue d'après un véhicule électrique.

b

c

b FISCHER Open and closed cars, each 20.5cm (7.9in). Two lightly constructed lithographed cars featuring adjustable steering.

b FISCHER Offener und überdachter Wagen, beide 20,5cm. Zwei leicht gebaute und bedruckte Spielzeug-autos mit verstellbarer Lenkung.

b FISCHER Voitures ouverte et fermée, 20,5cm chacune. Deux voitures à construction légère ayant une direction réglable.

c FISCHER Town coupé, 20.5cm (8.1in). The steering is adjustable, the leather roof can be folded up and down, and the windows slide open.

c FISCHER Coupé, 20,5cm. Die Lenkung ist verstellbar, das Lederverdeck kann geöffnet und geschlossen werden, und die Fenster können verschoben werden.

c FISCHER Coupé de ville décapotable, 20,5cm. La direction est réglable, le toit de cuir se replie en position fermée ou ouverte et les vitres à glissière s'ouvrent.

CARETTE Landaulette, 32cm (13in).
This elegant Carette Landaulette has
a rear folding leather hood, and two
opening doors.

CARETTE Landaulet, 32cm.
Dieser elegante Halblandauer von
Carette hat ein faltbares Lederdach
und zwei sich öffnende Türen.

CARETTE Landaulet, 32cm.
Cet élégant landaulet de Carette
comporte à l'arrière une capote à
soufflet en cuir et deux portes qui
s'ouvrent.

CARETTE Limousine, 40cm (15.7in).
Carette's most elaborate toy car,
which features fine handpainted
bodywork, four nickel-plated lights,
white rubber tyres, soldered wire
roofrack (the lithographed cars had
roofracks of pressed metal), bevelled
glass windows, heavily embossed
front seats, three side supports for the
running boards (as opposed to two
on the lithographed cars), and a
working steering wheel. The steering
is controlled by a ratchet mechanism
below the wheel. The driver is
plaster. This is the largest of three
sizes of this model.

CARETTE Limousine, 40cm.
Das vollkommenste Spielzeugauto
von Carette mit einem hübschen
handbemalten Aufbau, vier vernickelten Lampen, weißen Gummireifen,
einem Dachgepäckträger aus
vernickeltem Draht (die bedruckten
Wagen hatten gestanzte Gepäckträger), schrägen Glasfenstern, stark
geprägten Vordersitzen, drei Seiten-
stützen für die Trittbretter (im Gegensatz zu zweien bei den bedruckten
Ausführungen) und einem drehbaren
Lenkrad. Die Lenkung wird durch
einen Klinkenmechanismus unter dem
Rad betätigt. Der Fahrer besteht aus
Gips. Dies ist die größte Ausführung
des in drei Größen hergestellten
Modells.

CARETTE Limousine, 40cm.
C'est le jouet automobile de Carette
le plus sophistiqué, il se distingue par
sa carrosserie très bien peinte à la
main, quatre phares nickelés, des
pneus en caoutchouc blanc, une
galerie en fil de fer soudé (les
voitures lithographiées avaient en
général des galeries en métal
embouti), des fenêtres en verre
biseauté, des sièges avant gravés
en profondeur, trois supports latéraux
pour les marchepieds les voitures
lithographiées elles, n'en
comportaient que deux) et un volant
qui fonctionne. La direction est
commandée par un encliquetage
à crochet placé sous le volant. Le
conducteur est en plâtre. Ce modèle
est le plus grand des trois tailles
existantes.

CARETTE Landaulette, 32cm (12.6in).
An unusual variation on the common
Carette 32cm Limousine. It was made
as a taxi.

CARETTE Landaulet, 32cm.
Eine ungewöhnliche Abwandlung der
gewohnten 32cm Carette-Limousine.
Sie wurde als Taxi hergestellt.

CARETTE Landaulet, 32cm.
Version inhabituelle de la limousine
Carette ordinaire de 32cm. Elle fut
conçue pour être un taxi.

BING Military saloon, 32cm (12.6in).
This is an interesting variation on the
typical Edwardian Bing car. It was
produced in the early years of World
War I. It has a chauffeur, opening
doors, two side lamps, and a working
handbrake.

BING Militärlimousine, 32cm.
Eine interessante Abwandlung des
typischen edwardianischen Wagens
von Bing, der in den ersten Jahren
des I. Weltkriegs produziert wurde. Er
hat einen Chauffeur, sich öffnende
Türen, zwei Seitenleuchten und eine
funktionsfähige Handbremse.

BING Limousine, 32cm.
Voici une variante intéressante de la
voiture Edwardienne type, de Bing.
Elle fut fabriquée durant les premières
années de la première guerre
mondiale. Elle a un chauffeur, des
portes qui s'ouvrent, deux lanternes
latérales et un frein qui fonctionne.

BING 1912 Limousine, 33cm (13in). This has adjustable steering and two opening doors. The choice of colour for the lithography is interesting.

BING Limousine von 1912, 33cm. Die Limousine hat eine verstellbare Lenkung und zwei sich öffnende Türen. Interessant ist die Farbwahl für den Druck.

BING Limousine 1912, 33cm. Cette voiture a une direction réglable et deux portes qui s'ouvrent. Le choix des couleurs de la lithographie est intéressant.

HANS EBERL Limousine, 28cm (11in).
An attractive mid-sized Limousine
featuring opening rear doors, an
ornate roofrack, and adjustable
steering.

HANS EBERL Limousine, 28cm.
Eine attraktive Limousine mittlerer
Größe mit sich öffnenden Hintertüren,
einem verzierten Dachgepäckträger
und verstellbarer Lenkung.

HANS EBERL Limousine, 28cm.
Jolie limousine de taille moyenne
caractérisée par ses portes arrière
ouvrantes, une galerie ouvragée sur
le toit et une commande réglable.

BING Saloon cars, 21cm, 25cm and
25cm (8.3in, 9.8in and 9.8in). Three
variations on a Bing saloon car of
c1908. The righthand and centre cars
have white rubber tyres; the
righthand version is handpainted, the
centre one is lithographed, and the
smaller example on the left has
plainer lithography and plain tin
wheels. All have two opening doors
and brake lever. An unusual feature
of the centre car is a front-loading
battery to power the electric lights.

BING Limousinen, 21cm, 25cm und
25cm. Drei Abwandlungen einer
Bing-Limousine von ca. 1908. Die
Wagen rechts und in der Mitte
haben weiße Gummireifen. Der rechte
Wagen ist handbemalt, der in der
Mitte bedruckt, und die kleinere
Ausführung links ist einfacher
bedruckt und hat schlichte
Blechräder. Alle haben zwei sich
öffnende Türen und einen
Bremshebel. Ein ungewöhnliches
Merkmal des Wagens in der Mitte
ist eine von vorn eingesetzte Batterie
für die Scheinwerfer.

BING Limousines, 21cm, 25cm et 25cm. Trois variantes d'une voiture Bing à conduite intérieure des années 1908. Les modèles de droite et du milieu ont des pneus en caoutchouc blanc; la version de droite est peinte à la main, celle du centre est lithographiée et l'exemplaire le plus petit, sur la gauche, a une lithographie plus commune et de simples roues en tôle. Elles ont toutes, deux portes qui s'ouvrent et un levier de frein. La voiture du centre possède une caractéristique peu banale, elle est munie d'une pile placée à l'avant pour faire marcher les lumières électriques.

EBERL Saloon, 19cm (7.5in). This finely lithographed saloon by Hans Eberl of Nuremberg has opening doors.

EBERL Limousine, 19cm. Diese hübsch bedruckte Limousine von Hans Eberl aus Nürnberg hat sich öffnende Türen.

EBERL Limousine, 19cm. Limousine finement lithographiée par Hans Eberl de Nuremberg. Ses portes s'ouvrent.

a MÄRKLIN Open four-seater, 1909, 26cm (10.2in). This is handpainted, with rubber tyres. It features an elaborate steering mechanism beneath the car. The figures are not original.

a MÄRKLIN Offener Viersitzer, 1909, 26cm. Der Wagen ist handbemalt, hat Gummireifen und unter dem Wagenboden einen komplizierten Lenkmechanismus. Die Figuren gehören nicht zur Originalausstattung.

a MÄRKLIN Double phaéton, 1909, 26cm. Ce modèle est peint à la main, muni de pneus en caoutchouc. Il est caractérisé par un mécanisme de direction élaboré, placé sous le véhicule. Les figurines ne sont pas d'origine.

b BING Open two-seater, 25cm (9.8in). This handpainted two-seater is based on a contemporary Mercedes car.

b BING Offener Zweisitzer, 25cm. Der Wagen stützt sich auf einen zeitgenössischen Mercedes als Vorlage.

b BING Voiturette, 25cm. Voiturette à deux places peinte à la main, elle s'appuie sur un modèle de Mercédès contemporain.

b

a

c BING Open four-seater, 28cm (11in). This 1904 handpainted car features white rubber tyres, three headlights, and deeply embossed leather button-upholstery. It is the middle of three sizes, the largest of which features a central working headlight operating from a small methylated spirits burner.

c BING Offener Viersitzer, 28cm. Dieser handbemalte Wagen von 1904 hat weiße Gummireifen, drei Scheinwerfer und tief geprägte Lederpolster. Er ist der mittlere von drei Größen. Das größte Modell besitzt einen Mittelscheinwerfer, der mit Hilfe einer kleinen Spiritusflamme betrieben wird.

c BING Voiturette quatre-places ouverte, 28cm. Cette voiture peinte à la main, datant de 1904, est caractérisée par des pneus en caoutchouc blanc, trois phares et des boutons de capitonnage en cuir fortement enfoncés. C'est la taille intermédiaire des trois existantes. La plus grande était caractérisée par un phare central marchant à l'aide d'un petit réchaud à alcool à brûler.

c

a CARETTE Open four-seater, 20.5cm
(8.1in). A lithographed four-seater.
The steering is adjustable.

a CARETTE Offener Viersitzer,
20,5cm. Ein bedruckter Viersitzer mit
verstellbarer Lenkung.

a CARETTE Voiture quatre-places
ouverte, 20,5cm. Elle est lithographiée. La direction est réglable.

c BING Rear-entrance tonneau,
21cm (8.3in). This 1904 handpainted
toy car has white rubber tyres, a
handbrake, and an operable steering
wheel. There is a small opening rear
door to enable the rear passengers
to enter.

c BING Rückeinstiegwagen, 21cm.
Dieses handbemalte Spielzeugauto
von 1904 hat weiße Gummireifen,

a

c

b

b CARETTE Open two-seater, 15cm
(5.9in). A small, simple lithographed
car featuring glass windscreen,
simple pressed wheels and a flywheel
mechanism.

b CARETTE Offener Zweisitzer, 15cm.
Ein kleiner, schlicht bedruckter
Wagen mit Glaswindschutzscheibe,
einfachen Stanzmetallrädern und
einem Schwungradmechanismus.

b CARETTE Voiturette, 15cm.
Simple petite voiture lithographiée
munie d'un pare-brise en verre, de
roues simplement enbouties et d'un
mécanisme de volant à synergie.

eine Handbremse und ein drehbares
Lenkrad. Eine kleine sich öffnende
Hecktür dient für den Einstieg der
Fondpassagiere.

c BING Tonneau à entrée arrière,
21cm. Ce jouet automobile peint à la
main date de 1904, il a des pneus en
caoutchouc blanc, un frein à main et
un volant qui fonctionne. Il est muni
d'une petite porte arrière qui s'ouvre
pour permettre aux passagers
d'entrer à l'arrière.

BING Saloon, 27cm (10.2in).
A superior quality handpainted model with glazed windows, two opening doors, rubber tyres, brake, and adjustable steering.

BING Limousine, 27cm.
Ein handbemaltes Modell in hervorragender Qualität mit Glasscheiben, zwei sich öffnenden Türen, Gummireifen und verstellbarer Lenkung.

BING Limousine, 27cm.
Modèle de haute qualité, peint à la main, muni de vitres, de deux portes qui s'ouvrent, de pneus en caoutchouc, d'un frein et d'une direction réglable.

BING Open four-seater, 19cm (7.5in). c1908. This car is handpainted, with adjustable steering, rubber tyres and handbrake.

FISCHER Town coupé, 19cm (7.5in). The steering is adjustable, and the car has an operable brake. The two lamps are not original.

FISCHER Coupé, 19cm. Der Wagen ist lenkbar und hat eine funktionierende Bremse. Die beiden Lampen sind nicht original.

FISCHER Coupé de ville, 19cm. La direction est réglable et la voiture a un frein qui marche. Les lanternes ne sont pas d'origine.

BING Offener Viersitzer, 19cm. Der etwa aus dem Jahre 1908 stammende handbemalte Wagen hat eine verstellbare Lenkung, Gummireifen und eine Handbremse.

BING Voiturette quatre-places ouverte, 19cm. Fabriquée en 1908, cette voiture est peinte à la main, elle a une direction réglable, des pneus en caoutchouc et un frein à main.

c CARETTE Saloon, 32cm (12.6in). This is the middle size of a range of three. It has two opening doors, rubber tyres, glass windows, adjustable steering and a brake lever.

c CARETTE Limousine, 32cm. Dies ist die mittlere Größe der dreiteiligen Reihe. Sie hat zwei sich öffnende Türen, Gummireifen, Glasfenster, eine verstellbare Lenkung und einen Bremshebel.

c CARETTE Limousine, 32cm. Taille intermédiaire d'une série de trois. Elle a deux portes qui s'ouvrent, des pneus de caoutchouc, des vitres en verre, une conduite réglable et un levier de frein.

a

b

a GÜNTHERMANN Town convertible, 23cm (9.1in). An attractive town convertible by Günthermann, featuring white rubber tyres, high quality lithography, and a handpainted driver.

a GÜNTHERMANN Kabriolett, 23cm. Ein attraktives Kabriolett von Günthermann mit weißen Gummireifen, hochwertigem Druck und einem handbemalten Fahrer.

a GÜNTHERMANN Décapotable de ville, 23cm. Plaisante voiture décapotable Günthermann, caractérisée par des pneus en caoutchouc blanc, une haute qualité de lithographie et un conducteur peint à la main.

b GÜNTHERMANN Saloon, 19cm (7.5in). The interesting key drive – through one of the rear wheels – is almost unique.

b GÜNTHERMANN Limousine, 19cm. Der interessante Antrieb – über eines der Hinterräder – ist fast einmalig.

b GÜNTHERMANN Limousine, 19cm. L'intéressante commande à clef, à travers une des roues arrière, est presque unique en son genre.

GÜNTHERMANN Open four-seat tourer, 40cm (15.7in). An interesting and rare car. It is handpainted, with four lamps, four opening doors, and an adjustable glass windscreen. It was originally sold with four plaster figures, located on spikes on the seats.

HESS Open four-seater, 24.5cm (9.7in). The flywheel mechanism in this Hess four-seater is wound from the front handle.

HESS Offener Viersitzer, 24,5cm. Der Schwungradmechanismus dieses Viersitzers von Hess wird mit der Kurbel von vorn aufgezogen.

HESS Double phaéton, 24,5cm. Le volant à synergie dont cette quatre-places Hess est munie se remonte à l'aide de la poignée avant.

GÜNTHERMANN Offener viersitziger Tourenwagen, 40cm. Ein interessanter und seltener Wagen. Er ist hand-bemalt und hat vier Scheinwerfer, vier sich öffnende Türen und eine verstellbare gläserne Windschutzscheibe. Er wurde ursprünglich mit vier Gipsfiguren verkauft, die mit Dornen auf den Sitzen befestigt waren.

GÜNTHERMANN Double phaéton, 40cm. Rare et intéressante voiture. Elle est peinte à la main, comporte quatre phares, quatre portes ouvrantes et un pare-brise réglable en verre. A l'origine elle était vendue avec quatre figurines en plâtre, fixées sur des pointes émergeant des sièges.

GÜNTHERMANN Open four-seat tourer, 29cm (11.4in). This simple and rather plain car was probably manufactured at the end of the period, c1912. It features four opening doors and a lithographed driver. A clockwork motor drives the rear axle. The key is the simulated crank handle.

GÜNTHERMANN Offener viersitziger Tourenwagen, 29cm. Dieser einfache und recht schlichte Wagen wurde wahrscheinlich um 1912 hergestellt. Er hat vier sich öffnende Türen und einen bedruckten Fahrer. Ein Federwerk treibt die Hinterachse an. Der Aufziehschlüssel ist die simulierte Anlasserkurbel.

GÜNTHERMANN Double phaéton, 29cm. Cette voiture simple et plutôt laide, fut probablement fabriquée à la fin de la période, vers 1912. Elle se caractérise par quatre portes qui s'ouvrent et un conducteur litho-graphié. Un moteur mécanique commande l'essieu arrière. La clef simule une manivelle.

HESS Open two-seater and four-seater, 22.5cm and 23cm (8.9in and 9.1in). Both cars feature lithographed artillery wheels, flywheel drives, and original plaster chauffeurs.

HESS Offener Zweisitzer und Viersitzer, 22,5cm und 23cm. Beide Wagen haben bedruckte Speichenräder, Schwungradantriebe und ursprünglich aus Gips hergestellte Fahrer.

HESS Voitures ouvertes, deux et quatre-places, 22,5 et 23cm. Ces deux voitures sont caractérisées par des roues d'artillerie lithographiées, un volant à synergie et des conducteurs en plâtre, d'origine.

HESS Rear entrance tonneau, 23cm (9.1in). A flywheel-driven, steerable four-seater. The driver is not original.

HESS Wagen mit Rückeinstieg, 23cm. Ein durch ein Schwungrad angetriebener lenkbarer Viersitzer. Der Fahrer gehört nicht zur Originalausstattung.

HESS Tonneau quatre-places à entrée arrière, 23cm. Actionné par un volant à synergie, dirigeable. Le conducteur n'est pas d'origine.

FISCHER Two open four-seaters, both 22cm (8.7in). Fine lithographed tinplate simulates upholstery; the steering is adjustable; and on the lefthand car, the folding front windscreen is glazed.

FISCHER Zwei offene Viersitzer, beide 22cm. Die Polsterung wird durch sorgfältig bedrucktes Blech simuliert. Die Lenkung ist verstellbar, und die abklappbare Windschutzscheibe des linken Wagens besteht aus Glas.

FISCHER Double phaétons, 22cm chacun. En fer blanc finement lithographié à l'imitation du capitonnage; leur direction est réglable et le pare-brise repliable de la voiture de gauche est vitré.

Maker unknown Saloon, 22.5cm (8.9in). Possibly by Richter & Co, this appears to be a four-seat open tourer over which a simple tin roof has been fixed.

Hersteller unbekannt Limousine, 22,5cm. Dieser möglicherweise von Richter & Co hergestellte Wagen scheint ursprünglich ein offener Vier-sitzer zu sein, auf den ein schlichtes Blechdach aufgesetzt wurde.

Fabricant inconnu. Conduite intérieure, 22,5cm. Il s'agit peut-être de Richter & Co, cette voiture semble être une torpédo à laquelle on a simplement ajouté un toit de fer blanc.

FISCHER Open four-seater, 21cm (8.3in). The key is unusually placed, directly under the clockwork mechanism. The windscreen is glazed, and the steering is adjustable.

FISCHER Offener Viersitzer, 21cm. Der Schlüssel hat eine ungewöhnliche Position – direkt unter dem Federwerk. Die Windschutzscheibe besteht aus Glas, und die Lenkung ist verstellbar.

FISCHER Double phaéton, 21cm. La clef a une place inhabituelle, elle est placée directement sous le mécanisme. La vitre de devant est en verre et la direction est réglable.

FISCHER Saloon, 30cm (11.8in).
A simple lithographed Limousine,
featuring two opening doors,
adjustable steering, and a clockwork
mechanism.

FISCHER Limousine, 30cm.
Eine schlichte bedruckte Limousine mit
zwei sich öffnenden Türen, verstellbarer Lenkung und einem Federwerk.

FISCHER Limousine, 30cm.
Simple limousine lithographiée,
caractérisée par deux portes qui
s'ouvrent, une direction réglable et un
mouvement mécanique.

b BURNETT and BUB? Saloon cars, 36cm, 34cm and 34cm (14.2in, 13.4in and 13.4in). Right, a lithographed German tin car; centre, a deluxe handpainted version of the same vehicle featuring white rubber tyres; both believed to be by Karl Bub. They have opening windscreens. The car on the left is a very similar, though simplified, lithographed car by Burnett Ltd of England. This does not have an opening glass windscreen.

b BURNETT und BUB, Limousinen, 36cm, 34cm und 34cm. Rechts: ein bedrucktes deutsches Blechspielzeug-auto. Mitte: eine handbemalte Luxusausführung des gleichen Grundmodells mit weißen Gummi-reifen. Beide Wagen, deren Windschutzscheiben aufstellbar sind, werden Karl Bub zugeschrieben. Links: ein sehr ähnliches, wenn auch vereinfachtes bedrucktes Auto von Burnett Ltd. aus England. Es besitzt keine ausstellbare Windschutzscheibe.

b BURNETT et BUB? Limousine et conduites intérieures, 36cm, 34cm et 34cm. A droite: voiture allemande en tôle lithographiée. Au centre: version de luxe du même véhicule, peint à la main, caractérisé par des pneus en caoutchouc blanc; on pense que ces deux modèles seraient de Karl Bub. Ils ont des pare-brise qui s'ouvrent. La voiture de gauche est très similaire, bien qu'il s'agisse d'une voiture lithographiée simplifiée de Burnett Ltd.; Angleterre. Cette dernière n'a pas de pare-brise ouvrant.

a

a Maker unknown Limousine, 26.7cm (10.5in). Despite its many Carette-like features, most collectors believe that this commonly found, pre-World War I tin toy car was made by Karl Bub. No original pre-1914 Bub catalogue has been seen, so this cannot be conclusively proved.

a Hersteller unbekannt Limousine, 26,7cm. Trotz der vielen an Carette erinnernden Merkmale halten die meisten Sammler dieses bekannte, vor dem I. Weltkrieg hergestellte Blechspielzeugauto für ein Erzeugnis von Karl Bub. Da es jedoch keinen Bub-Katalog aus dieser Zeit gibt, bleibt diese Vermutung unbewiesen.

a Fabricant inconnu. Limousine, 26,7cm. En dépit de ses traits de ressemblance avec Carette, la majorité des collectionneurs pense que cette petite voiture de tôle communément répandue avant la première guerre mondiale, fut fabriquée par Karl Bub. On ne peut cependant le prouver de façon concluante, aucun catalogue Bub original antérieur à 1914 n'ayant jamais été trouvé.

bedruckte Limousine, rechts eine Krankenwagenversion, auf deren Haube die Halterung für die heute fehlende Flagge sichtbar ist.

Fabricant: probablement BUB, environ 1912, chaque voiture 26cm. Celle de gauche est une limousine lithographiée, celle de droite une ambulance. On peut voir qu'un abattant manque sur le capot de cette dernière.

BUB, Limousine, 33cm.
Le fabricant est presque certainement
Karl Bub. La voiture est lithographiée
et se caractérise par des portes
arrière qui s'ouvrent, deux grands
phares munis de verre, un conducteur
lithographié et des roues à gros
rayons dites: d'artillerie.

BUB, Limousine 1912, 19cm (7.5in).
A simplified and smaller version of
the previously illustrated car.

BUB, Limousine, 1912, 19cm.
Eine vereinfachte und kleinere
Ausführung des zuvor abgebildeten
Wagens.

BUB, Limousine 1912, 19cm.
Version simplifiée plus petite de la
voiture illustrée précédemment.

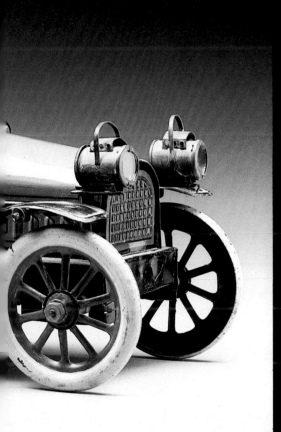

b BING Saloon taxi, 42cm (16.5in). The detail of this impressive handpainted taxi includes a working steering wheel and taximeter. It has rubber tyres, glass window, and four opening doors.

b BING Taxi-Limousine, 42cm. Details dieses eindrucksvollen handbemalten Taxis sind ein drehbares Lenkrad und ein Taxameter. Die Taxe hat Gummiräder, ein Glasfenster und vier sich öffnende Türen.

b BING Taxi à conduite intérieure, 42cm. Les accessoires de cet étonnant taxi peint à la main, comprennent un volant qui fonctionne et un taximètre. Il a des pneus en caoutchouc, des vitres en verre et quatre portes qui s'ouvrent.

a

a FISCHER Taxi, 30cm (11.8in). The folding roof is leather; there is a static meter mounted on the side of the vehicle. The front of the radiator has been restored.

a FISCHER Taxi, 30cm. Das Faltverdeck besteht aus Leder, und an der Seite ist ein Taxameter befestigt. Das Frontblech wurde restauriert.

a FISCHER Taxi-landaulet, 30cm. La capote arrière ouvrante est en cuir, un compteur fixe est monté sur le côté du véhicule. L'avant du radiateur a été restauré.

b

GREPPERT & KELCH, LEHMANN Two taxis, 19cm and 17.5cm (7.5in and 6.9in). These taxis reveal the influence of the American yellow cab. The left-hand cab is made by Greppert & Kelch of Brandenburg, and has two opening doors and adjustable steering. The other is by Lehmann and has a coil-spring mechanism.

GREPPERT & KELCH, LEHMANN Zwei Taxis, 19cm und 17,5cm. Diese Taxis lassen den Einfluß der typischen amerikanischen gelben Taxen erkennen. Das linke stammt von Greppert & Kelch aus Brandenburg und hat zwei sich öffnende Türen und eine verstellbare Lenkung. Das andere stammt von Lehmann und wird von einem Spiralfederwerk angetrieben.

GREPPERT ET KELCH, LEHMANN Deux taxis, 19cm et 17,5cm. Ces taxis révèlent l'influence des taxis jaunes américains. Le taxi de gauche est une fabrication Greppert et Kelch de Brandenbourg, il a deux portes qui s'ouvrent et une direction réglable. L'autre est une fabrication Lehmann, il est muni d'un mécanisme de ressort à spirale.

FISCHER Taxi, 17cm (6.7in). This lithographed taxi has a leather folding roof.

FISCHER Taxi, 17cm. Dieses bedruckte Taxi hat ein Faltverdeck aus Leder.

FISCHER Taxi-landaulet, 17cm. Ce taxi lithographié a un toit ouvrant en cuir.

LEHMANN Two convertibles, 17.5cm and 16.5cm (6.9in and 6.5in). The 'Berolina' (EPL 686) has adjustable steering, brake, and a folding cloth roof.

LEHMANN Zwei Kabrioletts, 17,5cm und 16,5cm. Der „Berolina" (EPL 686) hat eine verstellbare Lenkung, Bremse und ein Faltverdeck aus Stoff.

LEHMANN voitures décapotables, 17,5cm, 16,5cm. La "Berolina" (EPL 686) a une direction réglable, un frein et une capote de tissu qui se replie.

LEHMANN Two versions of 'Panne' (EPL 687),.each 16.5cm (6.5in). This open four-seater has adjustable steering.

LEHMANN Zwei Versionen der „Panne" (EPL 687), beide 16,5cm. Dieser offene Viersitzer hat eine verstellbare Lenkung.

LEHMANN Deux versions de la "Panne" (EPL 687) 16,5cm chacune. Ces double phaétons ont une direction réglable.

STOCK 'Chatt chatt', 20cm (7.9in). This ingenious open four-seater is one of Stock's few automobiles, as the firm specialized in novelty toys. The man waves his hat and an engine-noise is simulated mechanically, hence the name. The car can be steered from the wheel.

STOCK „Chatt chatt", 20cm. Dieser ausgeklügelte offene Viersitzer ist eines der wenigen Autos der Fa. Stock, die sich auf Neuheiten und Modespielzeug spezialisiert hatte. Der Mann schwenkt seinen Hut, und mit mechanischen Mitteln wird das Motorengeräusch simuliert – daher der Name. Der Wagen ist mit dem Lenkrad steuerbar.

STOCK "Chatt chatt", 20cm. Cette ingénieuse quatre-places ouverte est l'une des rares voitures de Stock, cette firme étant plus spécialisée dans les jouets de nouveauté. L'homme agite son chapeau et le bruit du moteur est imité mécaniquement, d'où son nom. La voiture peut être conduite par le volant.

'KBN' Open car, 17cm (6.7in). The letters 'KBN' stamped on the back indicate that the maker is Karl Bub. However, it is shown in the 1911 Carette catalogue, offered with tinplate driver or, as in this example, a cloth-dressed driver with tinplate face. It appears that Bub took over the pressings when Carette ceased production in 1917, which might also explain the Carette-like quality of other Bub cars from this period. The gear lever controls the car's backwards-and-forwards motion.

"KBN" Voiturette, 17cm. Les lettres "KBN" imprimées à l'arrière indiquent que le fabricant est Karl Bub. Pourtant elle est reproduite au catalogue Carette de 1911, proposée avec un conducteur en fer blanc ou, comme c'est le cas ici, un conducteur habillé de tissu, au visage en fer blanc. Il semble que Bub reprit l'estampage quand Carette cessa sa production en 1917; ce qui expliquerait également la qualité Carette d'autres jouets automobiles Bub de cette époque. Le levier de vitesse commande le mouvement avant-arrière du véhicule.

"KBN" Offener Wagen, 17cm. Die auf der Rückseite eingestanzten Buchstaben "KBN" deuten auf Karl Bub als Hersteller hin. Der Wagen wird jedoch im Carette-Katalog von 1911 mit einem Blechfahrer oder, wie in dieser Abbildung, mit einem in Stoff gekleideten Fahrer mit Blechge-

LEHMANN 'Tut-tut' (EPL 490), 17cm (6.7in). One of Lehmann's most famous novelty toys. The fat man blows his trumpet, perhaps representing an early road-hog. A cam drives the steering and this in turn moves the man's right arm. Simultaneously, a bellows produces an approximate trumpet sound.

LEHMANN "Tut-tut" (EPL 490), 17cm. C'est l'une des plus célèbres innovations de Lehmann. Le gros homme fait marcher sa trompe, il imite peut-être un des premiers chauffards. Un arbre à came commande la direction et anime ensuite le bras droit du personnage. Simultanément, un soufflet produit une sorte de coup de klaxon.

sicht angeboten. Vermutlich übernahm Bub die Stanzteile oder Stanzmuster, als Carette 1917 die Produktion einstellte. Dies würde auch die an Carette erinnernden Merkmale anderer Bub-Autos aus dieser Zeit erklären. Der Gangschalthebel regelt die Vor- und Rückwärtsfahrt des Wagens.

LEHMANN „Tut-tut" (EPL 490), 17cm. Eine der berühmtesten Neuheiten Lehmanns. Der dicke Mann bläst seine Trompete und stellt vielleicht einen ersten Verkehrsrowdy dar. Eine Nocke steuert die Lenkung, die ihrerseits den rechten Arm des Mannes bewegt. Ein Balg erzeugt zur gleichen Zeit einen trompetenähnlichen Ton.

GÜNTHERMANN 'Gordon Bennett', 30cm (11.8in). A representation of a competitor in the Gordon Bennett Cup motor race. Its raking line was complemented by the original figures (missing here) crouched into the wind. The tyres are rubber, and chain-driven by clockwork. Beneath the car, miniature bellows produce a hooting sound to warn bystanders as the car roars past.

GÜNTHERMANN „Gorden Bennett", 30cm. Nachbildung eines Teilnehmers am Autorennen um den Gordon-Bennett-Pokal. Die abfallende Linie wurde durch die hier fehlenden Figuren ergänzt, die sich gegen den Wind beugten. Die Gummiräder werden über eine Kette vom Aufzieh-werk angetrieben. Miniaturbälge unter dem Wagen produzieren bei rasanter Fahrt ein Hupgeräusch zur Warnung der Fußgänger.

GÜNTHERMANN "Gordon Bennet", 30cm. Modèle réduit d'un des concurrents de la coupe Gordon-Bennet. La pente de sa ligne se continuait grace aux figurines d'origine (absentes ici), tapies pour se protèger du vent. Les pneus sont en caoutchouc et mécaniquement animés par une chaîne. En dessous de la voiture des soufflets miniatures avertissent les piétons par des coups de klaxon, de son passage.

HESS Racing car, 13cm (5.1in). This racer is flywheel-driven. The aggressive figure adds a touch of dynamism.

HESS Rennwagen, 13cm. Dieser Rennwagen wird von einem Schwungrad angetrieben. Die aggressiv aussehende Figur gibt dem Wagen eine dynamische Note.

HESS Voiture de course, 13cm. Ce modèle a un volant à synergie. La figurine agressive qui l'accompagne ajoute une pointe de dynamisme.

HESS Racer, 20.5cm (7.9in).
An imaginatively posed figure
enhances this flywheel-driven racer.

HESS Rennwagen, 20,5cm.
Eine phantasievoll eingesetzte Figur
unterstreicht den Charakter dieses
schwungradgetriebenen Rennwagens.

HESS Coureur, 20,5cm.
La position pleine d'imagination
donnée à la figurine, met en valeur
ce coureur. L'ensemble est actionné
par un volant à synergie.

a GÜNTHERMANN Two-seat racing car, 16cm (6.3in). One of the smaller-sized Günthermann racing cars, featuring an enthusiastic driver and mechanic, a clockwork mechanism, and lithography of superb quality.

a GÜNTHERMANN Zweisitziger Rennwagen, 16cm. Einer der kleineren Rennwagen von Günthermann mit einem entschlossen blickenden Fahrer und einem Mechaniker, einem Federwerkantrieb und in überlegener Drucktechnik.

a GÜNTHERMANN Voiture de course deux places, 16cm. C'est l'une des plus petites voitures de course de Günthermann, qui se singularise par un conducteur et un mécanicien enthousiastes, un mouvement à clef et une lithographie de qualité superbe.

b

b Maker unknown Racing car, 28cm (11in). This rubber-tyred racing car is another in the Gordon Bennett Cup style. It is probably German-made.

b Hersteller unbekannt Rennwagen, 28cm. Dieser gummibereifte Renn-wagen ist ein weiteres Modell im Stil des Gordon-Bennett-Pokals. Er wurde wahrscheinlich in Deutschland hergestellt.

b Fabricant inconnu. Voiture de course, 28cm. Cette voiture de course à pneus en caoutchouc est un autre exemple du style coupe Gordon-Bennet. Elle est probablement de fabrication allemande.

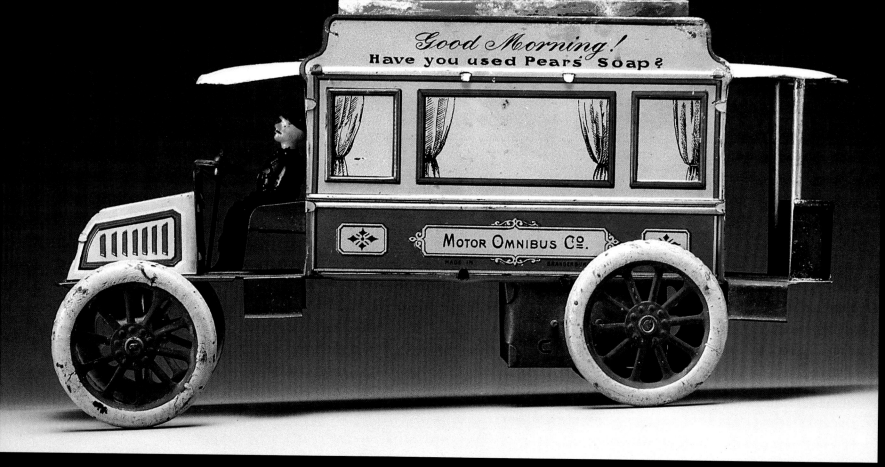

Good Morning!
Have you used Pears' Soap?

Motor Omnibus Co.

MADE IN BRANDENBURG

Maker unknown Motor omnibus, 26cm (10.2in). This omnibus has adjustable steering and features interesting and attractive lithography. The maker is possibly Oro of Brandenburg.

Hersteller unbekannt Motoromnibus, 26cm. Dieser Omnibus ist lenkbar und zeichnet sich durch einen interessanten und ansprechenden Druck aus. Der Hersteller ist wahrscheinlich Oro aus Brandenburg.

Fabricant inconnu. Omnibus à moteur, 26cm. Cet omnibus a une direction réglable et se caractérise par une belle et intéressante lithographie. Le fabricant pourrait être Oro de Brandenbourg.

BING Double-decker bus, 29cm
(11.4in). This bus (c1910) has
interesting lithographed
advertisements. The passengers are
Märklin figures. Steering is from the
wheel, there is an operable brake
lever, and the tyres are rubber.

BING Doppeldeckerbus, 29cm.
Dieser Bus (ca. 1910) trägt interessant
gedruckte Werbeaufschriften. Die
Passagiere stammen von Märklin. Die
Lenkung erfolgt mit dem Lenkrad. Der
Bus hat einen funktionsfähigen Brems-
hebel, die Reifen sind aus Gummi.

BING Omnibus à impériale, 29cm.
Cet omnibus, qui date d'environ
1910, porte d'intéressantes publicités
lithographiées. Les passagers sont
des figurines Märklin. Direction au
volant, le levier de frein fonctionne et
ses pneus sont en caoutchouc.

LEHMANN 'Autobus' (EPL 590), 21cm (8.3in). Lehmann was the first manufacturer to issue a version of the new omnibus. It was available in brown and white or red and white, and it features 'automatic spring arrest' and coil spring drive. The spring arrest system locked the motor as it was wound up, and released it when the car was put down; this avoided the need to hold the wheels.

LEHMANN „Autobus", (EPL 590), 21cm. Lehmann brachte als erster den neuen Autobus heraus. Er war in braun/weiß und rot/weiß erhältlich, hatte eine automatische Feder-arretierung und Spiralfederantrieb. Beim Aufziehen brauchten die Räder nicht festgehalten zu werden. Die Arretierung wurde beim Absetzen des Fahrzeugs freigegeben.

LEHMANN "Autobus" (EPL 590), 21cm. Lehmann fut le premier fabricant à sortir une version du nouvel omnibus. On le trouvait en marron et blanc ou en rouge et blanc, et sa particularité est "son ressort à arrêt automatique" et sa commande à ressort spirale. Le système d'arrêt du ressort bloquait le moteur pendant qu'on le remontait, et le libérait quand on reposait la

voiture, ce qui évitait d'avoir à retenir les roues.

RICHTER & CO Double-decker bus, c1910, 20.5cm (7.9in). A brightly lithographed small double-decker bus by this little known manufacturer.

RICHTER & CO Doppeldeckerbus, ca. 1910, 20,5cm. Ein farbenfroh bedruckter Doppeldeckerbus dieses wenig bekannten Herstellers.

RICHTER & CO. Omnibus à impériale, environ 1910, 20,5cm. Petit omnibus à impériale à lithographie brillante par ce fabricant peu connu.

BURNETT London bus, 23cm (9.1in).
This fine Burnett omnibus has
adjustable steering, a forward/
reverse action, and opening doors. It
was made c1920 and is based on the
typical London bus of that period.

BURNETT Londoner Autobus, 23cm.
Dieser hübsche Omnibus von Burnett
hat eine verstellbare Lenkung, Vor-
und Rückwärtsfahrt und sich öffnende
Türen. Er wurde ca. 1920 gebaut und
stützt sich auf den typischen
Londoner Autobus jener Zeit.

BURNETT Omnibus londonien, 23cm.
Ce bel omnibus Burnett a une
direction réglable, un mécanisme
avant-arrière et des portes qui
s'ouvrent. Il fut fabriqué vers 1920 et
s'inspire de l'omnibus londonien
classique de cette époque.

Makers unknown Two double-decker buses, each 21.5cm (8.5in). The makers of these attractively lithographed English-made buses are possibly Smith and Kavell, and if so, then they also manufactured the 'Minerva Series' which includes the Lyons Van, see page 140.

Hersteller unbekannt Zwei Doppeldeckerbusse, beide 21,5cm. Die Hersteller dieser attraktiv gestalteten englischen Omnibusse sind wahrscheinlich Smith und Kavell. In diesem Falle stammt auch die „Minerva-Reihe" mit dem Lyons-Lieferwagen (S.S. 140) von diesem Hersteller.

Fabricant inconnu. Omnibus à impériale, 21,5cm chacun. Les deux fabricants anglais de ces omnibus à ravissante lithographie sont peut-être Smith et Kavell et, dans ce cas, ils ont également fabriqué la "série Minerva" qui comprend la fourgonnette Lyons, voir page 140.

HESS Two-seat racing car, 16cm (6.3in). A middle-size brightly lithographed Hess racing car featuring goggled driver and typical Hess flywheel mechanism.

HESS Zweisitziger Rennwagen, 16cm. Ein mittelgroßer hellfarbig bedruckter Rennwagen von Hess mit einem Fahrer mit Schutzbrille und dem für Hess typischen Schwungradmechanismus.

HESS Voiture de course deux-places, 16cm. Voiture de course Hess de taille moyenne, brillamment lithographiée. Son conducteur à lunettes est particulier, de même que le volant à synergie typique de Hess.

HESS Truck, 25cm (9.8in).
The driver grasps a functioning
steering wheel. A flywheel provides
power.

HESS Pritschenwagen, 25cm.
Der Fahrer hält ein funktionierendes
Lenkrad. Der Antrieb kommt von
einem Schwungrad.

HESS Camion, 25cm.
Le conducteur tient un volant qui
fonctionne. Un volant à synergie lui
donne la puissance.

TIPP & CO Mail van and delivery van, 24.5cm and 24cm (9.6in and 9.4in). The Royal Mail van is a very early example by this manufacturer and was of course intended for the British market. The delivery van was for a Dutch department store.

TIPP & CO Postwagen und Lieferwagen, 24,5cm und 24cm. Der Postwagen ist ein sehr frühes Erzeugnis dieses Herstellers und war natürlich für den britischen Markt gedacht. Der Lieferwagen war für ein holländisches Kaufhaus bestimmt.

TIPP & CO, HESS Fourgon postal, et fourgonnette de livraison, 24,5 et 24cm. Le fourgon postal de la couronne est l'un des tous premiers modèles de ce fabricant. Il était destiné, bien entendu, au marché britannique. La fourgonnette fut fabriquée pour un grand magasin hollandais.

BRIMTOY/BING Royal Mail van, 29cm (11.4in). This Royal Mail van with opening rear door was produced for the British market.

BRIMTOY/BING Postzustellwagen, 29cm. Dieser Zustellwagen für die Royal Mail mit einer sich öffnenden Hecktür wurde für den britischen Markt hergestellt.

BRIMTOY/BING Fourgon postal, 29cm. Ce fourgon postal anglais muni d'une porte arrière qui s'ouvre, fut fabriqué pour le marché britannique.

LEHMANN 'Royal Mail' van (EPL 585), and 'La La' delivery van (EPL 620), each 18cm (6.7in). For the British market Lehmann created a solid English mail van which makes a striking contrast with the jauntily-decorated 'La La'. They both have adjustable steering and two opening doors.

LEHMANN Postwagen „Royal Mail" (EPL 585) und Lieferwagen „La La" (EPL 620), beide 18cm. Für den britischen Markt schuf Lehmann den soliden englischen Postzustellwagen, der einen starken Kontrast zum lebhaft geschmückten „La La" bildet. Der Postwagen ist lenkbar und hat zwei sich öffnende Türen. Beide Wagen haben eine verstellbare Lenkung und zwei sich öffnende Türen.

LEHMANN "Poste Royale" fourgon (EPL 585) et "La La" camion de livraison (EPL 620) 18cm chacun. Lehmann créa pour le marché britannique un solide fourgon postal qui suscite un contraste frappant avec la décoration cavalière de la "La La". Tous deux ont une direction réglable et deux portes qui s'ouvrent.

FISCHER Delivery lorry, 78cm (7.11n). This lorry was made for the English market, and features a rear-opening flap supported by chains, and a leather roof.

FISCHER Lieferwagen, 78cm. Dieser für den britischen Markt hergestellte Lieferwagen hat eine durch Ketten gehaltene sich öffnende Heckklappe und ein Lederverdeck.

FISCHER Camion de livraison, 78cm. Ce camion fut fabriqué pour le marché anglais, il se caractérise par un abattant qui s'ouvre à l'arrière, soutenu par des chaînes, et un toit bâché en cuir.

LEHMANN Two delivery vans, each 17cm (6.7in). Yellow and red variants of the Lehmann continental postal delivery van.

LEHMANN Zwei Lieferwagen, beide 17cm. Gelbe und rote Ausführungen des kontinentalen Postzustellwagens von Lehmann.

LEHMANN Deux camions de livraison, 17cm chacun. Variantes jaune et rouge du camion de livraison postal de Lehmann.

LEHMANN 'Aha' (EPL 550) and 'Caritas' ambulance (EPL 727), each 17cm (6.7in). Versions of the 'Aha' were available with and without driver. The 'Caritas' ambulance is very rare.

LEHMANN „Aha" (EPL 550) und Krankenwagen „Caritas" (EPL 727), beide 17cm. Der „Aha" war in Ausführungen mit und ohne Fahrer

erhältlich. Der Krankenwagen „Caritas" ist außerordentlich selten.

LEHMANN "Aha" (EPL 550) et ambulance "Caritas" (EPL 727), 17cm chacune. La "Aha" existait en option avec ou sans conducteur. L'ambulance "Caritas" est très rare.

LEHMANN Variant of 'Aha' (EPL 550), 17cm (6.7in). A very rare variant almost certainly made for advertising purposes; the trade mark on the side is lithographed over embossing. This is the only example of the variant so far recorded.

LEHMANN Variante des „Aha" (EPL 550), 17cm. Eine sehr seltene Variante, die mit ziemlicher Sicherheit für Werbezwecke hergestellt wurde. Das Warenzeichen auf der Seite wurde auf die Prägung aufgedruckt. Dies ist das einzige bisher bekannt gewordene Exemplar dieser Abwandlung.

LEHMANN Variante de la "Aha" (EPL 550), 17cm. Très rare variante, elle fut certainement fabriquée à des fins publicitaires; la marque apposée sur le côté est lithographiée sur l'estampage. C'est le seul exemplaire de cette variante répertorié jusqu'ici.

a LEHMANN Based on 'Lu Lu' (EPL 763), 19cm (7.5in). This delivery van has as an unusual feature a Chevrolet symbol on the front. The car is from a rare special issue made for the German department store Jandorf. The 'Lu Lu' was often produced to order with a particular firm's markings, for advertising purposes.

a LEHMANN Abwandlung des „Lu Lu" (EPL 763), 19cm. Dieser Lieferwagen hat als ungewöhnliches Merkmal ein Chevrolet-Emblem auf dem Kühler. Der Wagen ist ein Exemplar aus einer seltenen Serie, die für das deutsche Kaufhaus Jandorf hergestellt wurde. Der „Lu Lu" wurde oft im Auftrag mit den Farben oder Symbolen bestimmter Firmen für Werbezwecke hergestellt.

a LEHMANN Copie de "La La" (EPL 763), 19cm. Ce camion de livraison a un trait particulier; il porte un insigne Chevrolet à l'avant; cette voiture provient d'une série spéciale fort rare, faite pour le grand magasin allemand Jandorf. La "La La" fut surtout fabriquée sur commande à la marque de firmes particulières, à des fins publicitaires.

b

b LEHMANN 'Ihi' delivery van (EPL 595) and 'Salus' ambulance (EPL 734), each 18cm (6.7in). On the left is the 'Ihi', which was a fine model of a travelling shop, including working fabric roller curtains. The motor mechanism is fitted with auto arrest, as is that of the 'Salus' on the right. The 'Salus' is fitted with four revolving stretchers.

b LEHMANN Lieferwagen „Ihi" (EPL 595) und Krankenwagen „Salus" (EPL 734), beide 18cm. Links der „Ihi", ein hübsches Modell eines Verkaufswagens mit funktionsfähigen Rolljalousien aus Stoff. Der Antriebsmechanismus besitzt ebenso wie der des „Salus" eine automatische Arretierung. Der „Salus" ist mit vier rotierenden Bahren ausgerüstet.

b LEHMANN "Ihi" camion de livraison (EPL 595) Ambulance "Salus" 18cm chacun. A gauche le "Ihi" beau modèle de boutique ambulante, comprenant des stores en tissu s'enroulant et se déroulant. Le mécanisme du moteur est muni d'un auto-arrêt, comme celui du "Salus" reproduit à droite. Le "Salus" est muni de quatre tendeurs rotatifs.

a

LEHMANN 'Halloh' (EPL 683), 22cm. (8.7in). This motorcycle features a gyroscope mechanism for stability. It was also made as the Echo. It is interesting to note that early Hallohs feature a handpainted rider and lithographed motorcycle. Later versions had lithographed riders as well.

LEHMANN „Halloh" (EPL 683), 22cm. Dieses Motorrad besitzt einen Kreisel-mechanismus zur Erhaltung des Gleichgewichts. Es wurde auch als „Echo" hergestellt. Interessant ist, daß die frühen Modelle des „Echo" einen handbemalten Fahrer und eine bedruckte Maschine hatten. Bei späteren Ausführungen wurden auch die Fahrer bedruckt.

LEHMANN "Halloh" (EPL 683), 22cm. Cette motocyclette est stabilisée par un mécanisme gyroscopique. Elle fut également fabriquée sur le modèle de l"Echo". Il est intéressant de noter que les premières "Halloh" comportaient un motocycliste peint à la main et une motocyclette lithographiée. Les versions ultérieures comportent également des motocyclistes lithographiés.

LEHMANN 'Echo' (EPL 725) and 'Pilot' (EPL 726) motorcycles, both 22cm (8.7in). The 'Echo' is basically the same design as the 'Halloh', but replaces the gyroscope with a clockwork motor and small supporting wheels to maintain the balance. The 'Pilot' is a further variation on this useful design.

LEHMANN Motorräder „Echo" (EPL 725) und „Pilot" (EPL 726), beide 22cm. Das Motorrad „Echo" hat die gleiche Grundausführung wie das „Halloh", besitzt aber anstelle des Kreisels ein Federwerk und kleine Stützräder zur Erhaltung des Gleich-gewichts. Der Typ „Pilot" ist eine weitere Abwandlung der gleichen erfolgreichen Vorlage.

LEHMANN "Echo" (EPL 725) et "Pilot" (EPL 726) Motocyclettes, 22cm chacune. L"Echo" est faite sur le même modèle que la "Halloh" mais comprend un moteur mécanique à la place du gyroscope et des roulettes d'appoint pour maintenir l'équilibre. Le "Pilot" est une autre variante de ce modèle.

LEHMANN 'Mars' (EPL 471), 13cm (5.1in). This clockwork motorcycle was sold separately from the "Anxious Bride", see next page.

LEHMANN „Mars" (EPL 471), 13cm. Dieses uhrwerkgetriebene Dreirad wurde auch separat verkauft. Das gleiche Dreirad wurde beim Spielzeug „Die ängstliche Braut" als Zugdreirad verwendet.

LEHMANN "Mars" (EPL 471), 13cm. Cette motocyclette à clef était vendue séparément de la "mariée émue", voir page suivante.

LEHMANN 'Anxious Bride' (EPL 470), 23cm (9in). As this tricycle moves along, the woman brings a handkerchief to her eyes.

LEHMANN "mariée émue" (EPL 470), 23cm. Quand ce tricycle avance, la jeune femme porte un mouchoir à ses yeux.

LEHMANN „Die ängstliche Braut" (EPL 470), 23cm. Während der Fahrt des Motorrads verdeckt die Frau ihre Augen mit einem Taschentuch.

GREPPERT & KELCH Motorcycle and sidecar, 17cm (6.7in). Made c1910.

GREPPERT & KELCH Seitenwagen-gespann, ca. 1910, 17cm.

GREPPERT & KELCH Motocyclette et side-car, 17cm. Fabriquée vers 1910.

FISCHER Motorcycle with sidecar, 19cm (7.5in).

FISCHER Motorrad mit Seitenwagen, 19cm.

FISCHER Motocyclette avec side car, 19cm.

MOSES KOHNSTAM? Motorcycle,
20.5cm (7.9in). Probably by Moko,
this motorcycle has a flywheel drive.

MOSES KOHNSTAM? Motorrad,
20,5cm. Dieses wahrscheinlich von
Moko stammende Motorrad besitzt
einen Schwungradantrieb.

MOSES KOHNSTAM? Motocyclette,
20,5cm. Probablement fabriquée par
Moko, cette motocyclette est
actionnée par un volant à synergie.

FISCHER Motorcycle, 20cm (7.9in).
The design of this clockwork
lithographed motorcycle appears to
have been influenced by Lehmann's
'Echo'.

FISCHER Motorrad, 20cm.
Dieses mit einem Federwerk verse-
hene bedruckte Motorrad schien von
Lehmanns „Echo" beeinflußt worden
zu sein.

FISCHER Motocyclette, 20cm.
La forme de cette motocyclette
lithographiée à mouvement
mécanique semble avoir été inspirée
par celle de l"Echo" de Lehmann.

FISCHER Motorcycle, 18cm (7in).
A Fischer clockwork motorcycle with
passenger.

FISCHER Motorrad, 18cm.
Ein Aufzieh-Motorrad mit Soziusfahrer
von Fischer.

FISCHER Motocyclette, 18cm.
Motocyclette Fischer à mouvement
mécanique avec un passager.

GÜNTHERMANN Motorcycle, 18cm
(7in). An interesting motorcycle by
Günthermann, with a clockwork
motor and sparks created by the
mechanism.

GÜNTHERMANN Motorrad, 18cm.
Ein interessantes Motorrad von
Günthermann mit einem Federwerkantrieb, der gleichzeitig Funken
erzeugte.

GÜNTHERMANN Motocyclette,
18cm. Intéressante motocyclette de
Günthermann munie d'un moteur à
mouvement mécanique qui fait des
étincelles.

Maker unknown Motorcycle, 16cm
(6.3in). A clockwork lithographed
motorcycle possibly distributed by
Moko.

Hersteller unbekannt Motorrad, 16cm.
Ein möglicherweise von Moko
vertriebenes bedrucktes Motorrad mit
Federwerkantrieb.

Fabricant inconnu. Motocyclette,
16cm. Motocyclette lithographiée à
mouvement mécanique. Elle fut peut-
être distribuée par Moko.

WK Motorcycle with sidecar, 18cm
(7in). This motorcycle combination
was made for the British market; note
the Automobile Association insignia
on the sidecar.

WK Motorrad mit Seitenwagen,
18cm. Dieses Seitenwagengespann
wurde für den britischen Markt hergestellt. Man beachte die Initialen der
Automobile Association auf dem
Seitenwagen.

WK Motocyclette avec side car,
18cm. Cet ensemble fut conçu pour
le marché britannique; notez l'insigne
de l'Association Automobile placé sur
le side car.

1918-1930

Die technischen Entwicklungen in den Jahren nach dem Ersten
Weltkrieg ermöglichten den Herstellern die Produktion sehr ins
Detail gehender Nachbildungen echter Vorlagen. Hersteller wie
E. P. Lehmann steckten erhebliche Summen in den Patentschutz für
Vorrichtungen, die Geräusche erzeugten, Spielzeuge zu
Bewegungen ähnlich Lebewesen befähigten oder neue
Antriebsformen ermöglichten und in viele andere Neuerungen.

Zu den technischen Erfindungen und Neuerungen kamen neue
Druckverfahren, der Einsatz neuer Werkstoffe zur Verbesserung
des Aussehens des fertigen Autos und die Beibehaltung der
charakteristischen Merkmale bestimmter Hersteller. Die besten
Spielzeugautos aus dieser Zeit sind eher Interpretationen als
Kopien ihrer echten Vorbilder.

1918-1930

Le développement de la technologie au cours de années qui ont
suivi la première guerre mondiale a permis aux fabricants
de jouets de créer des reproductions extrêmement détaillées
de véhicules authentiques. Des fabricants tels que E.P. Lehmann
investirent des fonds considérables pour breveter des mécanismes
capables de produire des sons et d'animer les jouets, ils rendirent
possibles de nouvelles méthodes de propulsion, et bien d'autres
innovations.

Ces découvertes technologiques allaient de pair avec de nouveaux
procédés lithographiques, l'utilisation de matériaux différents
destinés à améliorer la finition de l'objet, tandis que s'imposait
la personnalité du fabricant. Les meilleurs modèles de petites
voitures fabriqués pendant cette période interprètent plus qu'ils
ne copient leurs originaux.

1918-1930

The development of technological skills in the years after the First World War allowed the toymakers to create highly detailed representations of real cars. Manufacturers such as E P Lehmann invested considerable sums in patenting devices which created sounds, animated the toys, enabled new methods of propulsion and many other innovations.

The technological discoveries were accompanied by new methods of lithography, the use of different materials to enhance the finished car, and a retention of the maker's personality. The best toy cars of the period interpret rather than copy their originals.

MÄRKLIN Open touring car, 30cm (11.8in). A rarity from the 1920s; few examples have been found. The driver is not original. The car is handpainted.

MÄRKLIN Offener Tourenwagen, 30cm. Eine Seltenheit aus den zwanziger Jahren, die in nur wenigen Exemplaren erhalten ist. Der Fahrer des handbemalten Wagens gehört nicht zur Originalausstattung.

MÄRKLIN Voiture de tourisme ouverte, 30cm. Rare voiture des années 1920. On en a trouvé peu d'exemples. Le conducteur n'est pas d'origine. La voiture est peinte à la main.

METALGRAF Town coupé, 24cm (9.5in). This Italian-made car has movable front steering, a clockwork mechanism activated by a key at the back, and a rear axle set at an angle so that it will run in a circle.

METALGRAF Coupé, 24cm. Dieses italienische Auto hat eine verstellbare Vorderradlenkung, einen durch einen hinten eingesteckten Schlüssel betätigten Federmechanismus und eine in einem Winkel zur Vorderachse montierte Hinterachse, so daß der Wagen im Kreise fährt.

METALGRAF Coupé de ville, 24cm. Cette voiture de fabrication italienne a une direction avant amovible, un mouvement mécanique actionné par une clef placée à l'arrière et un essieu arrière fixé à un tourillon de façon à tourner en cercle.

MÄRKLIN Saloon car, 30cm (11.8in).
This is the saloon version of the open
tourer on this page. It has three
opening doors, a handbrake, an
adjustable windscreen, and is
handpainted.

MÄRKLIN Limousine, 30cm.
Dies ist die Limousinenausführung des
offenen Tourenwagens auf dieser
Seite. Sie hat drei sich öffnende
Türen, eine Handbremse, eine verstellbare Windschutzscheibe und ist
handbemalt.

MÄRKLIN Conduite intérieure, 30cm.
Voici la version conduite intérieure de
la torpédo reproduite sur cette page.
Elle a trois portes qui s'ouvrent, un
frein à main et un pare-brise
réglable, elle est peinte à la main.

a FISCHER Closed coupé, 25cm (9.9in). This interesting coupé features two opening doors and a rear dicky seat. It has electric lights and a rear stop light as well. It was manufactured in the 1920s and on into the 1930s.

a FISCHER Geschlossenes Coupé, 25cm. Dieses interessante Coupé hat zwei sich öffnende Türen und einen hinteren Notsitz. Es besitzt elektrische Scheinwerfer einschließlich einer Rückleuchte. Es wurde in den zwanziger und dreißiger Jahren hergestellt.

a FISCHER Coupé fermé, 25cm. Cet intéressant coupé a deux portes qui s'ouvrent et un spider. Il a un éclairage électrique et également un stop à l'arrière. Il fut fabriqué des années 1920 aux années 1930.

c BUB Saloon, 42cm (16.5in). This car features three opening doors, adjustable windscreen and steering.

c BUB Limousine, 42cm. Dieser Wagen hat drei sich öffnende Türen, eine verstellbare Windschutzscheibe und eine bewegliche Lenkung.

a

b

c

b GÜNTHERMANN Open four-seat tourer, 26cm (10.25in). This is an interestingly shaped and lithographed open touring car, believed to have been made by Günthermann in the late 1920s. It has two headlights and adjustable steering.

b GÜNTHERMANN Offener viersitziger Tourenwagen, 26cm. Ein interessant gestalteter und bedruckter offener Tourenwagen, der wahrscheinlich von Günthermann Ende der zwanziger Jahre gebaut wurde. Er hat zwei Scheinwerfer und eine verstellbare Lenkung.

b GÜNTHERMANN Double phaéton, 26cm. Cette voiture de tourisme ouverte et lithographiée, a une forme intéressante. On pense qu'elle fut fabriquée à la fin des années 1920. Elle est munie de deux phares et d'une direction réglable.

c BUB Conduite intérieure, 42cm. Cette voiture a trois portes qui s'ouvrent, une pare-brise et une direction règlables.

a CARDINI Town coupé, 20.5cm (8.1in). An Italian-made lithographed coupé featuring headlights, adjustable steering, a chauffeur and a clockwork mechanism.

a CARDINI Coupé, 20,5cm. Ein in Italien gebautes bedrucktes Coupé mit Scheinwerfern, verstellbarer Lenkung, einem Chauffeur und einem Federwerkantrieb.

a CARDINI Coupé de ville, 20,5cm. Coupé lithographié de fabrication italienne possédant des phares, une direction réglable, un chauffeur et un mouvement mécanique.

c FISCHER Two saloon cars, 40cm and 33cm (15.75in and 13in). Two interesting Fischer saloon cars from the 1920s. Both have four opening doors and are lithographed. The steering is adjustable. Interestingly, only the smaller car has headlights.

a

c

b

b BUB Open four-seat tourer, 33cm (13in). This is another lithographed car by Karl Bub, with white rubber tyres, two opera lights at the side, and two small headlights. It has a glass windscreen, a brake lever, and a smartly-dressed chauffeur.

b BUB Offener viersitziger Tourenwagen, 33cm. Ein weiterer bedruckter Wagen von Karl Bub. Er hat weiße Gummireifen, zwei seitliche Suchscheinwerfer, zwei kleine Hauptscheinwerfer, eine gläserne Windschutzscheibe, einen Bremshebel und einen schmuck gekleideten Chauffeur.

b BUB Double phaéton, 33cm. Voici un autre exemple de voiture Karl Bub lithographiée. Elle est munie de pneus de caoutchouc blanc, de deux lanternes sur le côté et de deux phares. Elle a un pare-brise en verre, un levier de frein et un chauffeur habillé de façon élégante.

c FISCHER Zwei Limousinen, 40cm und 33cm. Zwei interessante Limousinen von Fischer aus den zwanziger Jahren. Beide sind bedruckt und haben vier sich öffnende Türen. Die Lenkung ist verstellbar. Auffallend ist, daß nur der kleinere Wagen Scheinwerfer hat.

c FISCHER Conduites intérieures, 30 et 33cm. Deux modèles intéressants de conduites intérieures Fischer des années 1920. Ils ont tous deux quatre portes qui s'ouvrent et sont lithographiés. La direction est réglable. Curieusement, seule la plus petite voiture possède des phares.

119

BUB Saloon, 30cm (11.8in).
This attractive car from the mid-1920s features the typical Bub lithographed disc wheels of the period. The original Karl Bub tag indicates that it was possibly a showroom model. The car is clockwork with adjustable steering.

BUB Limousine, 30cm.
Dieses attraktive Auto aus der Mitte der zwanziger Jahre ist in für Bub typischer Weise mit bedruckten Scheibenrädern versehen. Der originale Karl Bub-Anhänger deutet an, daß es möglicherweise ein Vorführmodell war. Der Wagen hat ein Federwerk und eine verstellbare Lenkung.

BUB Conduite intérieure, 30cm.
Cette voiture attirante du milieu des années 1920 possède des roues lithographiées en forme de disque caractéristiques de Bub à cette époque. L'étiquette Karl Bub d'origine semble indiquer qu'il s'agirait d'un modèle de vitrine. La voiture est à mouvement mécanique et conduite réglable.

b HESS Open and saloon cars, 18cm, 19.5cm and 21.5cm (7in, 7.7in and 8.5in). The lefthand car is a two-seat open tourer, that in the centre a four-seat open tourer, and that on the right, a limousine. All are on the same chassis and lithographed in typical Hess fashion though less attractively than the earlier Hess cars.

b HESS Offene Wagen und Limousinen, 18cm, 19,5cm und 21,5cm. Der linke Wagen ist ein zweisitziger offener Tourenwagen, der in der Mitte ein ähnlicher Viersitzer und der rechts eine Limousine. Alle haben das gleiche Fahrgestell und sind in der für Hess charakteristischen Weise, wenn auch weniger attraktiv als frühere Hess-Wagen, bedruckt.

b HESS Voitures ouvertes et conduites intérieures, 18cm, 19,5cm et 21,5cm. A gauche, voiture de tourisme à deux places ouverte, au centre, torpédo et à droite, limousine. Elles ont toutes le même châssis et sont lithographiées d'une manière particulière à Hess bien que de façon moins jolie que les premières voitures Hess.

d HESS Saloon, 23.5cm (9.25in). This lithographed Hess saloon has the typical flywheel mechanism, and two opening rear doors. It is a larger limousine than usual and quite a rare piece.

d HESS Limousine, 23,5cm. Diese bedruckte Hess-Limousine besitzt den charakteristischen Schwungradmechanismus und hat

a

b

a DISTLER Saloon, 35cm (13.75in). This car features a windscreen that moves forwards, a side-mounted spare wheel and quite fine lithography for the period, which is the late 1920s. Its electric lights were operated from a battery underneath the car. It has two opening doors.

a DISTLER Limousine, 35cm. Dieser Wagen hat eine nach vorn ausstellbare Windschutzscheibe, ein seitlich befestigtes Reserverad und ist in einer für die späten zwanziger Jahre hohen Qualität bedruckt. Die elektrischen Scheinwerfer wurden von einer Batterie unter dem Wagenboden gespeist. Zwei Türen lassen sich öffnen.

a DISTLER Conduite intérieure, 35cm. Cette voiture possède un pare-brise qui se lève en avant, une roue de secours montée sur le côté et une lithographie assez soignée pour l'époque, qui se situe à la fin des années 1920. Son éclairage électrique était alimenté par une pile située sous la voiture. Elle a deux portes qui s'ouvrent.

d

zwei sich öffnende Hintertüren. Sie ist größer als üblich und ein recht seltenes Exemplar.

d HESS Conduite intérieure, 23,5cm. Cette conduite intérieure Hess lithographiée a un volant à synergie type et deux portes qui s'ouvrent à l'arrière. C'est une limousine plus grande que la normale et une pièce fort rare.

c

c DISTLER Open tourer and saloon, each 31cm (12.2in). The open tourer features a rear luggage-rack, adjustable front windscreen, rack and pinion steering and opening rear doors. The saloon version features an opening toolbox on the running board and a luggage-rack (just visible at the rear). Both versions are lithographed and were made in the early 1920s.

c DISTLER Offener Tourenwagen und Limousine, beide 31cm. Der offene Tourenwagen hat einen Heckgepäckträger, eine verstellbare Windschutzscheibe, Zahnstangenlenkung und sich öffnende Hintertüren. Die Limousine besitzt einen zu öffnenden Werkzeugkasten auf dem Trittbrett und einen (hinten gerade noch sichtbaren) Gepäckträger. Beide Autos sind bedruckt und wurden Anfang der zwanziger Jahre hergestellt.

c DISTLER Voiture de tourisme ouverte et conduite intérieure, 31cm chacune. La voiture de tourisme ouverte est munie d'un porte-bagages arrière, d'un pare-brise réglable à l'avant, d'une direction à pignon, d'un râtelier et de portes arrières qui s'ouvrent. La version conduite intérieure possède une caisse à outils qui s'ouvre sur le marche-pied et un porte-bagages (visible seulement de l'arrière). Les deux modèles sont lithographiés et furent fabriqués au début des années 1920.

BING Saloon, 42cm (16.5in).
The deluxe version of the 40cm Bing
saloon on this page. It has finer
lithography, adjustable steering, a
glazed windscreen with sidelights,
and electric lights. The additional
length is accounted for by the
protruding bumper. Other details
characteristic of Bing are the two
opening doors, the spare wheel in
the rear, and the rubber tyres and
typically ingenious brake lever with
its forward and backward action. On
both cars the Bing trademark
appears beneath the radiator grille.

BING Limousine, 42cm.
Dies ist die Luxusausführung der 40cm
großen Bing-Limousine auf dieser
Seite. Sie ist sorgfältiger bedruckt, hat
eine verstellbare Lenkung, eine
gläserne Windschutzscheibe mit
Seitenlampen und elektrische Scheinwerfer. Die größere Länge ergibt sich
durch die vorstehende Stoßstange.
Weitere für Bing typische Details sind
die beiden sich öffnenden Türen, das
Reserverad hinten, die Gummireifen
und ein typischer, klug ersonnener
Bremshebel mit Vor- und Rückwärts-
verstellung. An beiden Wagen befindet sich das Firmenzeichen Bings
unter dem Kühler.

BING Conduite intérieure, 42cm.
Version de luxe de la conduite
intérieure de 40cm reproduite sur
cette page. Elle a une plus belle lithographie, une conduite réglable, un
pare-brise vitré muni de lanternes
latérales et d'un éclairage électrique.
Le pare-choc saillant ajoute à la
longueur. Les autres détails propres à
Bing sont les deux portes qui
s'ouvrent, les pneus de caoutchouc et
le levier de frein particulièrement
ingénieux avec son action avant et
arrière. La marque Bing est placée
derrière la grille du radiateur, sur les
deux modèles.

17cm (6.7in). The model on the left is a two-seater open coupé; that on the middle left a two-seater closed or 'doctor's' coupé; that on the middle right, a four-seater open tourer with hood up; that on the far right, a six-light limousine. It is interesting to note that the driver of the car on the far left is a lady.

Das linke Modell ist ein zweisitziges offenes Coupé, das in der Mitte links ein geschlossenes zweisitziges soge-nanntes „Ärztecoupé", das in der Mitte rechts ein offener Tourenwagen mit geschlossenem Verdeck und der Wagen ganz rechts eine Limousine mit sechs Scheinwerfern. Interessant ist, daß der Wagen ganz links von einer Dame gefahren wird.

17cm chacune. A gauche, coupé ouvert à deux places, au centre gauche coupé fermé à deux places dit "le docteur", au centre droite torpédo à capote relevée, à droite limousine à six phares. A noter la voiture qui se trouve à l'extrême gauche: elle est conduite par une femme.

BING Saloon, 40cm (15.75in). This lithographed saloon has two opening doors and adjustable steering. It features a typical Bing lithographed driver of the period, and beside it is a contemporary standard oil pump.

BING Limousine, 40cm.
Diese bedruckte Limousine hat zwei sich öffnende Türen und eine verstellbare Lenkung. Der bedruckte Fahrer ist typisch für die Erzeugnisse Bings in jener Zeit. Daneben eine zeitgenössische Zapfsäule.

BING Conduite intérieure, 40cm. Cette conduite intérieure litho-graphiée a deux portes qui s'ouvrent et une direction réglable. Son conducteur lithographié Bing est typique de cette époque. La pompe à huile standard placée à côté est contemporaine.

BUB Saloon, 28cm (11in).
This is a mid-1920s lithographed saloon which features an adjustable windscreen, two opera lights at the side, two headlights, opening doors, electric lights at the front, adjustable steering and a brake lever. Only the windscreen is glazed.

BUB Limousine, 28cm.
Diese bedruckte Limousine aus der Mitte der zwanziger Jahre hat eine verstellbare Windschutzscheibe, zwei seitliche Suchscheinwerfer, zwei Hauptscheinwerfer, elektrische Lampen vorne, verstellbare Lenkung und einen Bremshebel. Nur die Windschutzscheibe ist verglast.

BUB Conduite intérieure, 28cm.
Cette conduite intérieure lithographiée date du milieu des années 1920, elle a un pare-brise réglable, deux lanternes sur le côté, deux phares, des portes qui s'ouvrent, des lumières électriques à l'avant, une conduite réglable et un levier de frein. Seul le pare-brise est vitré.

DOLL ET CIE Steam-driven car, 48cm (19in). The boiler and mechanism are beneath the bonnet. The car features cast metal wheels with white rubber tyres, and a drive to the rear axle. The driver is not original.

DOLL ET CIE Dampfauto, 48cm.
Der Kessel und der Antriebsmechanismus befinden sich unter der Motorhaube. Der Wagen hat gegossene Räder mit weißen Gummireifen und Hinterradantrieb. Der Fahrer ist nicht original.

DOLL ET CIE Voiture à vapeur, 48cm.
Le chaudière et le mécanisme sont sous le capot. Cette voiture a des roues de métal embouti, des pneus de caoutchouc blanc et un essieu moteur arrière. Le conducteur n'est pas d'origine.

BING Open four-seater, 29cm (11.4in). This typical open four-seater has brake lever and adjustable steering.

BING Offener Viersitzer, 29cm.
Dieser typische offene Viersitzer hat einen Handbremshebel und eine bewegliche Lenkung.

BING Torpédo, 29cm.
Cette torpédo typique est munie d'un levier de frein et d'une direction réglable.

a MOSES KOHNSTAM Saloon, 25cm (9.9in). The name of the wholesaler, Moses Kohnstam, is abbreviated to 'Moko' on the radiator of this small lithographed green saloon. It has several interesting features, the most important of which is the centrally hinged bonnet which reveals an engine with working cylinders which move as the car is driven along by its clockwork motor.

a MOSES KOHNSTAM Limousine, 25cm. Der zu „Moko" abgekürzte Name des Großhändlers ist auf dem Kühler dieser kleinen bedruckten grünen Limousine wiedergegeben. Sie hat mehrere interessante Details, vor allem eine in der Mitte angeschlagene Motorhaube. Sie gibt einen Motor frei, dessen Zylinder sich bewegen, während der Wagen vom Federwerk angetrieben wird.

a MOSES KOHNSTAM Conduite intérieure, 25cm. Moko est l'abréviation du nom du grossiste, Moses Kohnstam, portée sur le radiateur de cette petite conduite intérieure verte, lithographiée. Elle comporte plusieurs particularités intéressantes dont la plus importante est le capot qui s'articule au centre pour découvrir un moteur muni de cylindres qui fonctionnent et bougent quand la voiture avance sous l'impulsion de son moteur à mouvement mécanique.

a

a

b BUB Open four-seat tourer, 29cm (11.4in). This open tourer of c1925 has a typical sporty 1920s look to it. It is lithographed and has a spare wheel at the side, opera lights beside the windscreen, a brake lever, and fixed steering. The wheels are of the solid disc type that became popular during the period.

b BUB Offener viersitziger Tourenwagen, 29cm. Dieser um 1925 hergestellte offene Tourenwagen folgt dem für die zwanziger Jahre typischen sportlichen Stil. Er ist bedruckt und hat ein Reserverad an der Seite, Suchscheinwerfer neben der Windschutzscheibe, einen Bremshebel und eine nicht verstellbare Lenkung. Die massiven Scheibenräder sind typisch für diesen Zeitabschnitt.

b BUB Double phaéton, 29cm. Cette voiture datant des années 1925 a un chic particulier aux années "folles". Elle est lithographiée, une roue de secours est fixée sur le côté. Une lanterne de chaque côté du pare-brise, un levier de frein, la direction est fixe. Les deux roues sont en forme de disques pleins en vogue à cette époque.

b

CITROËN B14 Saloon, 52cm (20.5in).
The largest Citroën of the series and
the only one in the Peter Ottenheimer
collection. It is a very realistic
handpainted car with a host of
features including frontwheel steering,
four opening doors, four windows
that slide up and down, a sun visor
above the windscreen, electric lights,
suspension; a significant toy of the
1920s.

CITROËN Limousine B14, 52cm.
Der größte Citroën der Reihe und der
einzige in der Sammlung Peter Otten-
heimers. Er ist ein sehr originalgetreu
handbemaltes Auto mit vielen technischen Details wie Vorderradlenkung,
vier sich öffnenden Türen, vier sich
auf- und abbewegenden Fenstern,
einer Sonnenblende über der
Windschutzscheibe, elektrischen
Lampen und einer Federung – eine
beachtliche Spielzeugentwicklung für
die zwanziger Jahre.

CITROËN B14. Conduite intérieure,
52cm. C'est la plus grande de toutes
les Citroën de série et la seule que
comprenne la collection Peter
Ottenheimer. C'est une voiture très
réaliste, peinte à la main, comportant
une foule de caractéristiques parmi
lesquelles des roues motrices avant,
quatre portes qui s'ouvrent, quatre
vitres qui montent et descendent, et
un pare-soleil au dessus du pare-
brise, un éclairage électrique, une
suspension. C'est un jouet important
des années 1920.

LEHMANN 'Baldur' (EPL 739), 27cm (10.6in). This is the taxi version of the 'Terra', using different lithography. It has no meter like the smaller Lehmann taxi, but it features the typical yellow and black American taxi colours.

LEHMANN „Baldur" (EPL 739), 27cm. Diese Taxiversion der „Terra" ist anders bedruckt. Sie hat keinen Taxameter wie das kleinere Lehmann-Taxi, ist aber in den typisch amerikanischen Taxifarben gelb und schwarz ausgeführt.

LEHMANN "Baldur" (EPL 739), 27cm. C'est la version taxi de la "Terra", elle est lithographiée de façon différente. Elle n'a pas de taximètre à l'inverse du taxi Lehmann de taille inférieure, mais porte les couleurs jaune et noire caractéristiques des taxis américains.

BUB Taxi version of saloon, 27cm (10.6in). This lithographed taxi is in American colours and was presumably intended for export to the United States. It features electric lights, clockwork mechanism, and adjustable steering.

BUB Taxiversion der Limousine, 27cm. Dieses Taxi ist in amerikanischen Farben bedruckt und war wahrscheinlich für den Export in die USA bestimmt. Es hat elektrische Scheinwerfer, ein Federwerk und eine verstellbare Lenkung.

BUB Version taxi d'une conduite intérieure, 27cm. Ce taxi lithographié a des couleurs américaines et fut probablement destiné à être exporté aux Etats-Unis. Il a des phares électriques, un mouvement mécanique et une direction réglable.

a LEHMANN 'Titania' (EPL 779), 25.5cm (10in). A middle-sized saloon with electric lights. The doors are simply lithographed onto the side panels and do not open.

a LEHMANN „Titania" (EPL 779), 25,5cm. Eine mittelgroße Limousine mit elektrischen Scheinwerfern. Die Türen sind lediglich auf die Seitenwände aufgedruckt und lassen sich nicht öffnen.

a LEHMANN "Titania" (EPL 779), 25,5cm. Conduite intérieure de taille moyenne à éclairage électrique. Les portes sont simplement lithographiées sur les panneaux latéraux, elles ne s'ouvrent pas.

c LEHMANN 'Lana' (EPL 776) and 'Brennabor' (EPL 777), each 18cm (7in). Two cars using the same chassis. The yellow and blue lithographed 'Lana' has plain headlights; the 'Brennabor' features electric lights and adjustable steering. Both have clockwork mechanisms.

a

b LEHMANN Open four-seat tourer (EPL 730), 25cm (9.9in). This is the 'Velleda'; it features two small additional folding seats at the front of the rear compartment, making this car in effect an optional six-seater. It was always issued in orange lithography as illustrated, and examples which still have the flag are uncommon. Unlike many Lehmann toys chiefly noted for their intricate mechanisms, the series of cars and vans had simple motors without strange or amusing features.

b LEHMANN Offener viersitziger Tourenwagen (EPL 730), 25cm. Dieser „Velleda" hat zwei zusätzliche Klapp-sitze hinten, so daß der Wagen bei Bedarf auch als Sechssitzer verwen-det werden kann. Er wurde immer orangefarben wie in der Abbildung verkauft, und Exemplare, die noch die Flagge besitzen, sind recht selten. Im Gegensatz zu vielen anderen für ihre ausgetüftelten Mechanismen bekann-ten Lehmann-Erzeugnissen haben die Personen-und Lieferwagen einfache Antriebe ohne besondere oder über-raschende Merkmale.

b LEHMANN Double phaéton (EPL 730), 25cm. Voici la "Velleda"; elle comporte deux petits strapontins supplémentaires à l'avant du compartiment arrière, ce qui fait de cette voiture en réalité une voiture six-places sur option. Elle fut toujours lithographiée orange comme ici, les modèles qui ont encore leur drapeau ne sont pas communs. A l'inverse de bien des jouets Lehmann, célèbres pour leurs mécanismes sophistiqués, les séries de voitures et de fourgon-nettes étaient munies de moteurs simples, sans caractéristique particulièrement étrange ou amusante.

c

b

c LEHMANN „Lana" (EPL 776) und „Brennabor" (EPL 777), beide 18cm. Zwei Wagen mit identischem Fahrgestell. Der gelb und blau bedruckte „Lana" hat imitierte Scheinwerfer, der „Brennabor" elektrische Scheinwerfer und eine verstellbare Lenkung. Beide haben Federwerke.

c LEHMANN "Lana" (EPL 776) et "Brennabor" (EPL 777), 18cm chacune. Deux voitures utilisant le même châssis. La "Lana" lithographiée bleu et jaune a des phares simples; la "Brennabor" a un éclairage électrique et une direction réglable. Elles sont toutes deux munies d'un mouvement mécanique.

d LEHMANN 'Luxus' (EPL 785) and 'Gala' (EPL 780), each 32cm (13in). These cars feature four opening doors; the 'Luxus' features electric lights, the 'Gala' has plain ones. They represent Lehmann's attempt to make a large car to rival those of Tipp & Co, Distler and Bub.

d LEHMANN "Luxus" (EPL 785) et "Gala" (EPL 780), 32cm chacune. Ces voitures ont quatre portes qui s'ouvrent; la "Luxus" a un éclairage électrique, la "Gala" a des phares simples. Elles concrétisent l'effort tenté par Lehmann de faire une grande voiture concurrente de celles de Tipp & Co, et de Distler et Bub.

d

d LEHMANN „Luxus" (EPL 785) und „Gala" (EPL 780), beide 32cm. Beide Wagen haben vier sich öffnende Türen. Der „Luxus" hat elektrische Scheinwerfer, der „Gala" nur Imitationen. Die Wagen zeugen von Lehmanns Bemühen, ein großes Auto in Konkurrenz zu Tipp & Co, Distler und Bub herzustellen.

Maker unknown Open four-seat car, 17.5cm (6.9in). This rare car is a model of a bullnosed Morris of the period. It has a clockwork mechanism. It bears the Moko mark, indicating that it was probably distributed by Moses Kohnstam.

Hersteller unbekannt Offener Vier-sitzer, 17,5cm. Dieses seltene Auto ist ein Modell eines Morris mit Rund-kühler jener Zeit. Es wird von einem Federwerk angetrieben. Das Auto trägt die Bezeichnung „Moko" und wurde wahrscheinlich von Moses Kohnstam verkauft.

Fabricant inconnu. Voiture à quatre places ouverte, 17,5cm. Cette rare voiture est un modèle Morris de l'époque. Elle a un mouvement mécanique. Elle porte la marque Moko, indiquant qu'elle fut probable-ment distribuée par Moses Kohnstam.

a LEHMANN Double garage (EPL 772) with small 'Galop' racing car (EPL 760) and the saloon car 'Sedan' (EPL 765), each 15cm (5.9in). The cars could be obtained separately, on their own or with a single garage.

b LEHMANN Two versions of 'Terra' (EPL 720), each 27cm (10.6in). The version with spoked wheels is the earlier.

b LEHMANN Zwei Versionen der „Terra" (EPL 720), beide 27cm. Die ältere ist die mit den Speichenrädern.

b LEHMANN Deux versions de "Terra" (EPL 720), 27cm. La version munie de roues à rayons est la plus ancienne.

a

b

a LEHMANN Doppelgarage (EPL 772) mit Kleinrennwagen „Galop" (EPL 760) und Limousine „Sedan" (EPL 765), beide 15cm. Die Autos wurden separat sowie mit und ohne Garage verkauft. Der Baum stammt nicht von Lehmann.

a LEHMANN Garage double (EPL 772), avec petite voiture de course "Galop" (EPL 760), et une conduite intérieure "Sedan" (EPL 765, 15cm chacune. On pouvait acheter ces voitures séparément, seules ou avec un garage à une place. L'arbre n'est pas de Lehmann.

c LEHMANN Two variations of 'Ito' (EPL 679), each 17cm (6.7in). The earlier of these two lithographed cars is the one with spoked wheels. The other followed after a few years.

c LEHMANN Zwei Varianten des „Ito" (EPL 679), beide 17cm. Der Wagen mit den Speichenrädern ist der ältere der beiden. Der andere wurde einige Jahre später hergestellt.

c LEHMANN Deux variantes de "Ito" (EPL 679), 17cm chacune. Celui qui porte des roues à rayons est le plus ancien de ces deux modèles lithographiés. L'autre le suit de quelques années.

c

TIPP & CO Londoner Autobus, 26,5cm.
Der Aufdruck sind typische Werbe-
beschriftungen der späten zwanziger
und frühen dreißiger Jahre. Dieses
Exemplar hat einen Federwerkantrieb,
Scheibenräder und eine verstellbare
Lenkung.

TIPP & CO. Autobus londonien,
26,5cm. Sa lithographie reproduit
deux publicités typiques de la fin des
années 1920 et du début des années
1930. Ce modèle a un moteur à
mouvement mécanique, des roues en
forme de disque et une conduite
réglable.

BURNETT Bus, 36cm (14.2in).
An interesting bus of fine lithography
incorporating adjustable steering.

BURNETT Autobus, 36cm.
Dieser interessante Autobus mit seiner
hohen Druckqualität hat eine
verstellbare Lenkung.

BURNETT Omnibus, 36cm.
Intéressant omnibus à belle
lithographie. Sa direction règlable est
incorporée.

ORO Two delivery vans, each 20cm (7.9in). Although these are cheerful, brightly lithographed vehicles, the quality of pressings and lithography is very much lower than that of Lehmann and several other German makers. It is interesting to note that though these vans are virtually identical, the lithography is different. The red van is probably slightly earlier because it features spoked wheels.

ORO Zwei Lieferwagen, beide 20cm. Obwohl diese Wagen farbenfroh und hell bedruckt sind, liegt die Druck-und Stanzqualität weit unter der Lehmanns und anderer deutscher Hersteller. Interessant ist, daß die Wagen zwar fast identisch sind, die Aufdrucke sich jedoch unterscheiden. Der rote Lieferwagen ist wahrscheinlich etwas älter, da er Speichenräder hat.

ORO Fourgonnettes de livraison, 20cm chacune. Bien qu'elles soient des voitures gaies, que leur lithographie soit haute en couleur, la qualité de l'estampage comme celle de la lithographie sont bien inférieures à celles de Lehmann ou de bien d'autres fabricants allemands. Il est intéressant de noter que nonobstant leur similitude, leur lithographie est différente. La fourgonnette rouge est probablement légèrement antérieure à cause de ses roues à rayons.

WELLS & CO Mail delivery van, 16cm (6.3in). This is a cheap lithographed mail van made in England in the late 1920s. It has two opening rear doors, a clockwork mechanism and adjustable steering. It lacks the finesse and quality of pressing of the German toys. This is particularly noticeable in the crudeness of the wheel spokes as compared to those in similar Lehmann vehicles of the period. However, the bright lithography and royal crest give the vehicle a certain charm.

WELLS & CO Postzustellwagen, 16cm. Dies ist ein billiger, bedruckter Postwagen, der Ende der zwanziger Jahre in England gebaut wurde. Er hat zwei sich öffnende Hecktüren, einen Aufziehmechanismus und eine verstellbare Lenkung. Ihm fehlen die Verfeinerung und Stanzqualität der deutschen Spielzeuge. Dies beweisen besonders die grob gearbeiteten Radspeichen, wenn man sie mit den Erzeugnissen Lehmanns aus der gleichen Zeit vergleicht. Die farbenfrohe Ausführung und das königliche Wappen verleihen dem Wagen jedoch seinen eigenen Charme.

WELLS & CO. Fourgon postal, 16cm. Ce fourgon postal vulgairement lithographié fut fabriqué en Angleterre à la fin des années 1920. Il a deux portes qui s'ouvrent, un mouvement mécanique et une direction réglable. Il n'a ni la finesse ni la qualité d'estampage des jouets allemands. C'est particulièrement visible dans la grossièreté d'exécution des rayons des roues, si on les compare à ceux des véhicules Lehmann similaires de cette époque. Pourtant la lithographie colorée et la couronne royale confèrent un certain charme à ce véhicule.

LEHMANN Delivery van, 14cm (5.5in).
This is a very rare Lehmann variation
on the common 'Sedan' (EPL 765),
lithographed with the mark of a shoe
retailing company, details of which
are to be seen on the roof.

LEHMANN Lieferwagen, 14cm.
Dies ist eine sehr seltene Lehmann-
Variation des gewohnten „Sedan"
(EPL 765). Der Aufdruck einer Schuh-
warenfirma ist auch auf dem Dach
sichtbar.

LEHMANN Fourgonnette de livraison,
14cm. Très rare variante de la
"Sedan" normale (EPL 765). Elle porte
la marque lithographiée d'un détail-
lant en chaussure, visible sur le toit.

English maker, unknown Steam lorry
and omnibus biscuit tins, both 18.5cm
(7.3in). Two brightly lithographed
English biscuit tins of the 1920s, with
good detail in the lithography.

England, Hersteller unbekannt Keksdosen als Dampflastkraftwagen und Omnibus, beide 18,5cm. Zwei farbenfroh und mit guter Detailausbildung bedruckte englische Keksdosen aus den zwanziger Jahren.

Fabricant anglais inconnu. Camion à vapeur et omnibus formant boîte à gâteaux, 18,5cm chacun. Deux boîtes à gâteaux anglaises des années 1920 lithographiées de façon vive et bien détaillée.

English maker, unknown Delivery truck biscuit tin, 24cm (9.5in). Another vehicle produced for advertising purposes. It has no mechanism.

England, Hersteller unbekannt Keksdose als Lastkraftwagen, 24cm. Ein weiteres für Werbezwecke bestimmtes Fahrzeug. Ein Antrieb ist nicht vorgesehen.

Fabricant anglais inconnu. Camion de livraison formant boîte à gâteaux, 24cm. C'est un autre véhicule fabriqué à des fins publicitaires. Il ne comporte pas de mécanisme.

LYONS'
CONFECTIONERY.

CATERERS BY APPOINTMENT TO
HIS MAJESTY THE KING & H·R·H·THE PRINCE OF WALES

BY APPOINTMENT

J. LYONS & Cº Lᵀᴰ·

BY APPOINTMENT

CADBY HALL, LONDON. W.14.

SECRETARY GEO. W. BOOTH.

English made, possibly by Smith and Kavell, 'Minerva Series', 18cm (7in). A finely lithographed, realistic British-made lorry. It has no clockwork mechanism. Undoubtedly there was an advertising link with Lyons, as other vehicles in the range carry advertisements from the same firm.

a England, "Minerva-Reihe", möglicherweise von Smith & Kavell, 18cm. Ein hübsch bedruckter originalgetreuer britischer Lastkraftwagen ohne Aufziehmechanismus. Zweifellos wurde für Lyons geworben, da auch andere Fahrzeuge dieser Reihe Werbeaufschriften für die gleiche Firma trugen.

a Fabricant anglais, peut-être Smith & Kavell, "série Minerva", 18cm. Camion de fabrication anglaise, réaliste et bien lithographié. Il ne comporte pas de mouvement mécanique. Faisait sans aucun doute l'objet d'accords publicitaires avec Lyons, car d'autres véhicules de cette gamme en arborent la publicité.

b LEHMANN 'Mensa' (EPL 688), 13cm (5.3in). This three-wheeled delivery vehicle has a rear opening door and features a simulated motor noise from the clockwork drive.

b LEHMANN „Mensa" (EPL 688), 13cm. Dieser dreirädrige Lieferwagen hat eine sich öffnende Hecktür. Das Federwerk erzeugt ein simuliertes Motorengeräusch.

b LEHMANN "Mensa" (EPL 688), 13cm. Ce véhicule de livraison à trois roues comporte une porte arrière qui s'ouvre et une direction à mouvement mécanique qui simule un bruit de moteur.

c LEHMANN 'Uhu' (amphibious car) (EPL 555), 26cm (10.25in). Another Lehmann creation. One of the least attractive of the novelty toys, and quite rare, possibly indicating that children did not find it appealing.

c LEHMANN Amphibienwagen „Uhu" (EPL 555), 26cm. Eine weitere Schöpfung von Lehmann und das am wenigsten ansprechende Neuheitenspielzeug. Seine Seltenheit kommt vielleicht daher, daß die Kinder dieses Spielzeug nicht mochten.

c LEHMANN "Uhu", voiture amphibie (EPL 555), 26cm. Autre création Lehmann. C'est l'une des nouveautés la moins réussie, elle est plutôt rare, ce qui semblerait indiquer qu'elle n'attira pas les enfants.

English, 19cm (7.5in).
A Macfarlane & Lang's biscuit tin
delivery van which features fine
lithography, with especially good
detail of the driver and his
companion. It has no mechanism.

England, 19cm.
Dieses als Keksdose dienende
Fahrzeug ist sorgfältig bedruckt, wie
die gut ausgeführten Details des
Fahrers und Beifahrers zeigen. Ein
Antrieb ist nicht vorgesehen.

Fabricant anglais, 19cm.
Fourgonnette de livraison formant
boîte à gâteaux Macfarlane & Lang
qui a une belle lithographie,
particulièrement soignée en ce qui
concerne le conducteur et son
compagnon. Il ne comporte pas de
mécanisme.

English, 24cm (9.5in).
A charming Huntley & Palmer biscuit
tin, with no motor, as is usually the
case with biscuit tin vehicles. Note
the fine detail in the lithography.

England, 24cm.
Eine hübsche Keksdose von Huntley
& Palmer. Wie bei den meisten als
Fahrzeuge ausgebildeten Keksdosen
ist kein Antrieb vorgesehen. Man
beachte die gute Ausführung des
Drucks.

Fabricant anglais Autobus anglais,
24cm. Charmante boîte à gâteaux
Huntley et Palmer. Elle ne comporte
pas de moteur comme c'est générale-
ment le cas des voitures boîtes à
gâteaux. Notez la finesse de détail
de la lithographie.

English, William Crawford's Rolls-Royce biscuit tin, 29cm (11.4in). A very accurate representation of a D-back Rolls-Royce of the 1920s. The figures are finely lithographed onto the windows. The roof of the vehicle opens, and to utilize as much of the interior as possible for storing the biscuits, no motor is provided.

England. William Crawfords Rolls-Royce als Keksdose, 29cm. Eine sehr genaue Nachbildung eines Rolls-Royce mit Steilheck aus den zwanziger Jahren. Die Figuren sind sorgfältig auf die Fenster gedruckt. Das Dach des Fahrzeugs läßt sich öffnen. Zur vollen Ausnutzung des Innenraums für die Aufbewahrung von Keksen wurde kein Federwerk vorgesehen.

Fabricant anglais. Rolls-Royce formant boîte à gâteaux William Crawford, 29cm. Modèle réduit très précis de la Rolls-Royce "D-back" des années 1920. Les figurines sont finement lithographiées sur les vitres. Le toit du véhicule s'ouvre et pour pouvoir utiliser autant d'espace intérieur que possible pour mettre des biscuits, le moteur a été supprimé.

a

b

b GEORGE LEVY Motorcycle with sidecar, 23cm (9in). A typical motorcycle combination by Levy.

b GEORGE LEVY Motorrad mit Seitenwagen, 23cm. Ein typisches Seitenwagengespann von George Levy.

b GEORGE LEVY Motocyclette avec side car, 23cm. Ensemble motocyclette type fabriqué par Levy.

a Maker unknown Motorcycle and sidecar, 24cm (9.5in). The maker of this combination, with police figures, has been thought to be George Levy.

a Hersteller unbekannt Motorrad mit Seitenwagen, 24cm. Als Hersteller dieses Seitenwagengespanns mit Polizisten wird George Levy vermutet.

a Fabricant inconnu Motocyclette à side car, 24cm. On pense que le fabricant de cet ensemble à figurines de policiers fut George Levy.

c CKO (KELLERMANN) Motorcycle, 16cm (6.3in). This motorcycle is a 'pushalong' toy without a mechanism.

c CKO (KELLERMANN) Motorrad, 16cm. Dieses Motorrad ist ein nur zum Schieben bestimmtes Spielzeug ohne Antrieb.

c CKO (KELLERMANN) Motocyclette, 16cm. Cette motocyclette est un jouet à pousser, sans mécanisme.

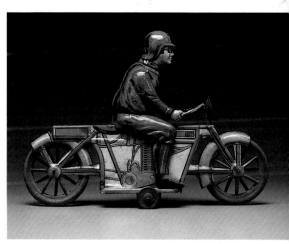

c

1930-1939

Die Jahre vor dem Zweiten Weltkrieg waren Jahre der Konsolidierung und des Wachstums. Die Produktionsverfahren für Blechspielzeugautos und die Unterhaltung großer Lagerbestände an Formen, Schablonen und Lehren begünstigten die Verwendung von Standardbauteilen, die als Grundbauteile für eine Vielzahl unterschiedlicher Spielzeuge eingesetzt wurden. Gleichzeitig reagierten die Spielzeughersteller auf die Vielfalt und Vielseitigkeit der echten Wagen auf den Straßen Europas und Amerikas.

Obwohl es in diesen Jahren einige herausragende Nachbildungen echter Vorlagen gab, die die Errungenschaften des Kraftfahrzeugbaus repräsentierten, waren Neuheitswert und phantasievolle Gestaltung noch immer wichtige Elemente bei den Spielzeugautos.

1930-1939

La seconde guerre mondiale a été précédée d'une période de consolidation et d'expansion. La méthode suivie pour construire les voitures en fer blanc, impliquant un stockage de réserves considérables de coquilles de moulages et de modèles, incita à généraliser l'emploi d'éléments standards. Ainsi les mêmes modules furent-ils utilisés pour la construction de base de toute une gamme de jouets différents, selon la façon dont les fabricants de jouet réagissaient à la diversité des automobiles grandeur nature qui sillonnaient les routes d'Europe et d'Amérique.

Bien que l'époque vit certaines répliques superbes de voitures réelles reflèter le degré de réussite auquel étaient parvenus les constructeurs automobiles, l'imagination et l'inventivité étaient toujours fortement présents dans les petites voitures.

1930-1939

The years before the Second World War were years of consolidation and expansion. The method of contruction of tin cars, involving the maintaining of large stocks of dies and patterns, encouraged a versatility in the use of the standard elements which saw the same components being used as the basis of a wide range of different toys, as the toymakers responded to the range and variety of real cars that were now travelling the roads of Europe and America.

Although the period saw some superb representations of real cars which reflected the achievements of the motor car manufacturers, novelty and fantasy were still strong elements in toy cars.

HESS Saloon, 21.5cm (8.5in).
This provides an interesting
comparison with the high quality,
detailed lithography of earlier Hess
cars. This version is much simpler and
cheaper, and does not have nearly
as much charm as those of the 1920s.
It features one opening door and can
move at different speeds.

HESS Limousine, 21,5cm.
Dieser Wagen läßt einen interessanten Vergleich zu den hochwertigen
und sorgfältig bedruckten älteren
Hess-Autos zu. Diese Ausführung ist
wesentlich einfacher und billiger, und
ihr fehlt vieles vom Charme der
Wagen aus den zwanziger und
dreißiger Jahren. Er hat eine sich
öffnende Tür und kann mit mehreren
Geschwindigkeiten fahren.

HESS Limousine à conduite intérieure,
21,5cm. Cette voiture permet une
comparaison intéressante avec la
grande qualité et le détail de la
lithographie des voitures Hess plus
anciennes. Cette version bon marché
est plus simple, elle a perdu le
charme de celles des années 1920.
Elle a une porte qui s'ouvre et peut
rouler à différentes vitesses.

in terms of lettering or Rolls-Royce patterning to the radiator.

an Rolls-Royce, jedoch gibt es keine weiteren von Rolls-Royce entlehnten Merkmale wie Beschriftungen oder Embleme auf dem Kühler.

Co. La grille du radiateur évoque fortement Rolls-Royce, bien qu'aucune marque ou insigne apposé à ce radiateur ne vienne le confirmer.

TIPP & CO Two-seater convertible, 32cm (13in). A charming two-seater with rear dicky seat, this was used in another guise as Tipp's Christmas car with a Father Christmas as driver. It is one of the few instances of a toy car with a lady driver; her costume, strongly reminiscent of the 1920s, is worth noting.

TIPP & CO Zweisitziges Kabriolett, 32cm. Ein hübscher Zweisitzer mit hinteren Notsitzen. In einer anderen Aufmachung wurde er als Tipps Weihnachtswagen mit einem Weihnachtsmann als Fahrer benutzt. Er ist einer der wenigen Wagen mit einer Fahrerin. Beachtenswert ist ihre Kleidung in der Mode der zwanziger Jahre.

TIPP & CO. Deux places décapotable, 32cm. Charmante deux-places avec spider arrière, elle servait à Tipp sous une autre forme de voiture de Noël avec un père Noël pour conducteur. C'est l'un des rares exemples de jouet automobile conduit par une femme; à noter la façon dont celle-ci est habillée, qui évoque fortement la mode des années 1920.

DISTLER Saloon, 32cm (13in). This saloon has two opening doors, electric headlight, stop light, adjustable steering, and backwards-and-forwards action. An unusual feature is that it has two motors.

DISTLER Limousine, 32cm. Diese Limousine besitzt zwei sich öffnende Türen, elektrische Scheinwerfer, Bremsleuchten, verstellbare Lenkung und fährt vorwärts und rückwärts. Ein ungewöhnliches Merkmal sind die zwei Antriebe.

DISTLER Conduite intérieure, 32cm. Cette conduite intérieure a deux portes qui s'ouvrent, des feux de stop, une direction réglable et un mouvement avant et arrière. Caractéristique inhabituelle: elle est équipée de deux moteurs.

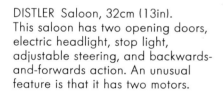

GÜNTHERMANN Tourer, 45cm
(17.7in). The folding roof is canvas;
there are four opening doors. The car
features electric lights.

GÜNTHERMANN Tourenwagen,
45cm. Der Wagen mit einem Lein-
wand-Rollverdeck hat vier sich
öffnende Türen und elektrische
Scheinwerfer.

DOLL ET CIE Open four-seater, 32cm
(13in). This rare handpainted car
features three opening doors, hand
brake, and adjustable steering.

DOLL ET CIE Offener Viersitzer, 32cm.
Dieser seltene handbemalte Wagen
hat drei sich öffnende Türen, eine
Handbremse und eine verstellbare
Lenkung.

DOLL ET CIE Double phaéton, 32cm.
Rare voiture peinte à la main. Elle a
trois portes qui s'ouvrent, un frein à
main et une direction réglable.

GÜNTHERMANN Voiture de
tourisme, 45cm. Le toit ouvrant est en
toile, les quatre portes s'ouvrent la
voiture est équipée d'un éclairage
électrique.

BUB Coupé, 39cm (15.4in).
This lithographed car features two
electric headlamps, two opening
doors, adjustable steering and an
outside brake lever.

BUB Coupé, 39cm.
Dieses bedruckte Auto hat zwei
elektrische Scheinwerfer, zwei sich
öffnende Türen, eine verstellbare
Lenkung und einen außen
angebrachten Bremshebel.

BUB Coupé à conduite intérieure,
39cm. Cette voiture lithographiée
possède deux phares électriques,
deux portes qui s'ouvrent, une
direction réglable et un levier de frein
extérieur.

a BUB Closed coupé, 30cm (11.8in).
This coupé by Karl Bub features
electric lights, brake lever, stop lights,
and the 'auto arrest' device which
facilitated winding the motor.

a BUB Geschlossenes Coupé, 30cm.
Dieses von Karl Bub stammende
Coupé hat elektrische Scheinwerfer,
Bremshebel, Bremsleuchten und die
automatische Arretierung beim
Aufziehen des Federwerks.

a BUB Coupé à conduite intérieure,
30cm. Ce coupé Karl Bub possède un
éclairage électrique, un levier de
frein, des feux de stop et un dispositif
d'arrêt qui facilitait le remontage du
moteur.

a

b MÄRKLIN Limousine, 39cm (15.4in).
This is one of the most attractive of
the range of Märklin constructor cars,
and one of the rarest, being made
only in the 1930s. It is handpainted,
though it lacks the quality of the
earlier cars. There were six in the
series, which included a coupé, a
lorry, a tanker, an armoured car, and
a racing car. The Limousine features
rubber tyres and spring suspension; it
was also available in beige and
green.

b MÄRKLIN Limousine, 39cm.
Dies ist eines der attraktivsten Autos
von Märklin und gleichzeitig eines
der seltensten. Es wurde nur in den
dreißiger Jahren hergestellt. Es ist
handlackiert, besitzt aber nicht die
Qualität älterer Wagen. Die Serie
bestand aus sechs Fahrzeugen, d.h.
einem Coupé, einem Lastwagen,
einem Tankfahrzeug, einem gepan-
zerten Wagen und einem Rennwagen. Die auch in beige und grün
hergestellte Limousine hat Gummireifen und eine Federung.

b MÄRKLIN Limousine, 39cm.
C'est l'une des plus belles voiture de
la gamme Märklin et l'une des plus
rares; elle ne fut fabriquée que dans
les années 1930. Elle est peinte à la
main, mais n'atteint cependant pas
la qualité des voitures antérieures.
La série comportait six voitures,
comprenant un coupé, un camion, un
camion-citerne, une voiture blindée,
et une voiture de course. La limousine
a des pneus de caoutchouc et une
suspension à ressort; elle existait
aussi en beige et en vert.

b

b BUB Saloon, 50cm (19.7in).
This very large lithographed saloon features adjustable steering, four opening doors, electric lights, and folding seats in the rear compartment. It is the largest saloon car made by this manufacturer at that period. One noteworthy feature is the prewar indicator which folds out from beside the windscreen.

b BUB Limousine, 50cm.
Diese übergroße bedruckte Limousine hat eine verstellbare Lenkung, vier sich öffnende Türen, elektrische Lampen und Klappsitze hinten und ist der größte von diesem Hersteller in jenen Jahren gebaute geschlossene Wagen. Auffallend ist der für die Vorkriegsmodelle typische ausklappbare Fahrtrichtungsanzeiger seitlich von der Windschutzscheibe.

b BUB Conduite intérieure, 50cm.
Cette conduite intérieure de grande taille, lithographiée, a une direction réglable, quatre portes qui s'ouvrent, un éclairage électrique et des sièges qui se rabattent à l'arrière. C'est la plus grande conduite intérieure conçue par ce fabricant à l'époque. Détail à noter; la flèche d'avant-guerre qui sort sur le côté du pare-brise.

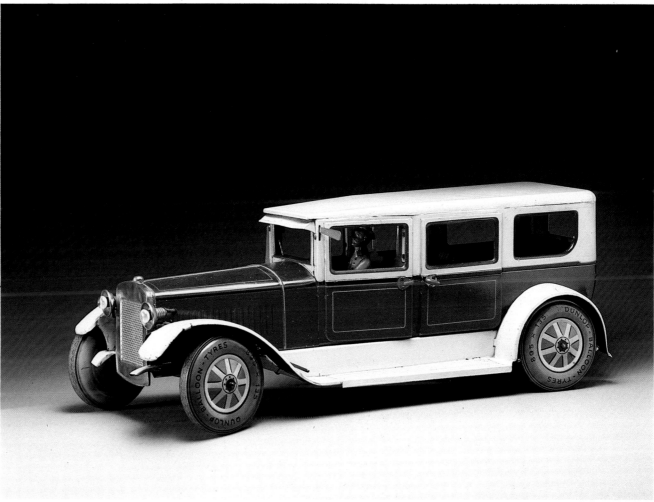

b

a BUB Convertible saloon, 27cm (10.6in). An extremely fine, very rare lithographed convertible by Karl Bub. It has electric lights and rubber tyres. It is an accurate model of the Horch 830BL of 1938. The windows can be raised and lowered, and the doors open. It is one of the more realistic tin toys of the 1930s.

a BUB Kabriolett, 27cm.
Ein außergewöhnlich hochwertiges und sehr seltenes Kabriolett von Karl Bub mit elektrischen Scheinwerfern und Gummireifen. Es ist eine original-getreue Nachbildung des Horch 830BL von 1938. Die Fenster lassen sich heben und senken, und die Türen lassen sich öffnen. Der Wagen ist eines' der vorlagentreueren Blech-spielzeuge der dreißiger Jahre.

a BUB Conduite intérieure décapotable, 27cm. Très rare et belle voiture décapotable Karl Bub, lithographiée. Elle est équipée d'un éclairage électrique et de pneus en caout-chouc. Elle reproduit fidèlement la Horch 830BL de 1938. Les vitres peuvent se lever et s'abaisser et les portes s'ouvrir. C'est l'un des jouets en fer blanc le plus réaliste des années 1930.

TIPP & CO The 'Hitler Mercedes', all 23cm (9in). Left and centre are two variations on the 'Hitler Mercedes'. These have rubber tyres and adjustable steering. Note particularly the detailed wheels and hub caps, the Mercedes emblem on the top of the radiator, and the detailed lights. This is an example of the developing sense of realism in Tipp toy cars of the late 1930s. On the right is the very rare coupé version of the same car, featuring two opening doors and the same details as on the two open cars.

TIPP & CO Drei Exemplare des „Hitler-Mercedes", alle 23cm. Links und in der Mitte zwei Abwandlungen des „Hitler-Mercedes" mit Gummireifen und verstellbarer Lenkung. Man beachte besonders die detailliert ausgebildeten Räder und Radnaben, den Mercedes-Stern auf dem Kühler und die detailliert ausgeführten Scheinwerfer. Sie beweisen den sich entwickelnden Sinn für Realität bei den Tipp-Spielzeugautos der späten dreißiger Jahre. Rechts die sehr seltene Coupéversion des gleichen Wagens mit zwei sich öffnenden Türen und den gleichen Details wie die beiden offenen Wagen.

TIPP & CO. "Mercédès d'Hitler", 23cm chaque. A gauche et au centre, variantes de la "Mercédès d'Hitler". Elles ont une direction réglable et des pneus de caoutchouc. A noter plus particulièrement le détail des roues et de leurs enjoliveurs, l'emblème Mercédès placé en haut du radiateur et le détail des lumières. Voici un exemple du réalisme qui se développa dans les petites voitures Tipp à la fin des années 1930. A droite, très rare version coupé de la même voiture. Ses deux portes s'ouvrent et elle a les mêmes détails que les deux voitures ouvertes.

TIPP & CO Two saloons, each 39cm
(15.4in). The righthand car features
electric lights and ajustable steering.

TIPP & CO Zwei Limousinen, beide
39cm. Der rechte Wagen hat
elektrische Scheinwerfer und eine
verstellbare Lenkung.

TIPP & CO. Conduites intérieures,
39cm chacune. La voiture de droite
possède un éclairage électrique et
une direction réglable.

TIPP & CO Coupé and saloon, each 52cm (20.5in). The coupé (on the right) features electric lights, adjustable steering, two opening doors, and an opening boot lid; the saloon is a simpler version.

TIPP & CO Coupé und Limousine, beide 52cm. Das Coupé (rechts) hat elektrische Lampen, eine verstellbare Lenkung, zwei sich öffnende Türen und einen zu öffnenden Gepäckraum-deckel. Die Limousine ist eine einfachere Ausführung.

TIPP & CO. Coupé et conduite intérieure, 52cm chacune. Le coupé, à droite, a un éclairage électrique, une direction réglable, deux portes qui s'ouvrent, de même que le coffre; la conduite intérieure est une version simplifiée.

TIPP & CO Mercedes 540K
'Autobahn-Kurier', 35cm (13.75in).
This outstanding lithographed toy
from the late 1930s is a remarkably
good replica of one of the glamorous
real cars of the period. The flowing
line of the rear wings has an almost
Art Deco quality. Technically and
artistically it is an impressive
achievement.

TIPP & CO Mercedes 540K
"Autobahn-Kurier", 35cm. Dieses
hervorragende bedruckte Spielzeug
aus den späten dreißiger Jahren
ist eine außergewöhnlich gute
Nachbildung eines der berühmten
Wagen jener Zeit. Die fließenden
Linien der hinteren Kotflügel haben
fast eine Art-Deco-Qualität. Das Auto
ist ein technisches und künstlerisches
Meisterwerk.

TIPP & CO. Mercédès 540K
"Autobahn-Kurier", 35cm. Cet
exceptionnel jouet lithographié
datant de la fin des années 1930, est
une réplique particulièrement fidèle
d'un fascinant modèle réel de
l'époque. La ligne plongeante des
ailes arrière rend bien l'esprit Art-
déco. Ce jouet réalise une prouesse
tant technique qu'artistique.

b BING Saloon, 48cm (19in).
One of the most remarkable cars of the 1930s, this features bright lithography of superb quality, with fine silver details. The 'KB' trademark of Karl Bub is to be found just above the 'BW' of Bing Werke. It appears to have been a joint venture, or possibly a car produced at the time of Bing's demise in the 1930s. This very large car has two opening doors and electric headlights.

b BING Limousine, 48cm.
Dieser Wagen, eines der herausragenden Erzeugnisse der dreißiger Jahre, zeichnet sich durch eine erstklassige Drucktechnik in hellen Farben und mit feinen Silberdetails aus. Das Firmenzeichen „KB" von Karl Bub befindet sich direkt über dem „BW" der Bing Werke. Er war entweder eine Gemeinschaftsproduktion oder aber ein Erzeugnis aus der Zeit des Niedergangs der Fa. Bing in den dreißiger Jahren. Dieser große Wagen hat zwei sich öffnende Türen und elektrische Scheinwerfer.

a TIPP & CO Saloon, 46cm (18.1in).
An elegant saloon with a large rear trunk. It has electric lights and adjustable steering. The colours are characteristic of Tipp & Co in the 1930s.

a

a TIPP & CO Limousine, 46cm.
Eine elegante Limousine mit einem großen Heckkofferraum. Sie hat elektrische Scheinwerfer und eine verstellbare Lenkung. Die Farben sind typisch für die Erzeugnisse von Tipp & Co in den dreißiger Jahren.

a TIPP & CO. Conduite intérieure, 46cm. Elégante conduite intérieure équipée d'une grande malle arrière. Elle a un éclairage électrique et une direction réglable. Les couleurs sont caractéristiques de Tipp & Co. dans les années 1930.

b BING Conduite intérieure, 48cm.
C'est l'une des voitures les plus remarquables des années 1930. Sa lithographie haute en couleur est de qualité superbe, rehaussée par de jolis détails argent. La marque "KB" de Karl Bub se trouve placée juste au-dessus du "BW" de Bing Werke. Il semble qu'il s'agisse d'une coproduction, ou bien d'une voiture fabriquée au moment de la cession de Bing dans les années 1930. Cette très grande voiture a deux portes qui s'ouvrent et un éclairage électrique.

DISTLER Petrol tanker, 28cm (11inh).
This tanker has adjustable steering.
Note the advertising emblem on the
side.

DISTLER Tankwagen, 28cm.
Dieser Tankwagen hat eine verstell-
bare Lenkung. Man beachte die
Werbung auf der Seite.

DISTLER. Camion-citerne à essence,
28cm. Camion-citerne à direction
réglable. A noter les logos publicitaires latéraux.

These vans from the Marseilles firm of André are based on the Peugeot 201 of the period. They have no mechanisms.

D ANDRÉ Lieferwagen, 17cm. Diese Lieferwagen der Fa. André aus Marseilles folgen dem Vorbild des Peugeot 201 jener Zeit. Sie haben keinen Antrieb.

D ANDRÉ Fourgonettes de livraison, 17cm. Ces fourgonettes de la firme marseillaise André sont copiées de la Peugeot 201 de l'époque. Elles n'ont pas de mécanisme.

(7.5in). This van has the lithography of the Deutsche Reichspost, which features the German eagle and swastika below, indicating that it was made when Hitler was in power during the 1930s. It has two rear opening doors and a roofrack. The same model was also produced without the swastika.

LEHMANN Postwagen (EPL 786), 19cm. Dieser Postwagen in den Farben der Deutschen Reichspost mit dem Reichsadler und dem Haken-kreuz darunter läßt erkennen, daß er während der Hitlerzeit in den dreißiger Jahren hergestellt wurde. Er hat zwei sich öffnende Hecktüren und einen Dachgepäckträger. Das gleiche Modell wurde auch ohne Hakenkreuz fabriziert.

LEHMANN Fourgon postal (EPL 786), 19cm. Ce fourgon est lithographié aux couleurs des postes du Reich allemand comprenant la croix gammée surmontée de l'aigle allemand. Cela indique qu'il fut fait pendant les années 1930, quand Hitler était au pouvoir. Les deux portes, situées à l'arrière du véhicule, s'ouvrent, le toit est équipé d'une galerie. Le même modèle était produit sans la croix gammée.

Continental maker (unknown) Single-decker omnibus biscuit tin, 19cm (7.5in). A characteristic biscuit tin creation of the period made for a Swiss biscuit factory.

Unbekannter kontinentaler Hersteller Keksdose als einstöckiger Omnibus, 19cm. Eine für jene Zeit charakteristische Ausführung einer Keksdose, die für eine schweizerische Bisquitfabrik hergestellt wurde.

Fabricant européen inconnu. Omnibus à un étage formant boîte à gâteaux, 19cm. C'est une création de boîte à gâteaux caractéristique de l'époque, pour une biscuiterie suisse.

CHAD VALLEY Delivery truck, 25cm (9.9in). An English-made van designed to advertise the range of Chad Valley games which can be seen lithographed all over the roof of the van. It is based on a 1930s Dennis and has immense charm and a high standard of lithography.

CHAD VALLEY Lieferwagen, 25cm. Ein in England hergestellter und zur Werbung für die Chad Valley-Spiele bestimmter Lieferwagen. Die gesamte Dachfläche wurde zur Werbung ausgenutzt. Das hübsch und ansprechend gestaltete Fahrzeug mit seiner hohen Druckqualität stützt sich auf einen Dennis von 1930 als Vorlage.

CHAD VALLEY. Camion de livraison, 25cm. Camion anglais conçu pour faire de la publicité pour les jeux de Chad Valley lithographiés sur tout le toit du camion. Elle a pour modèle une voiture Dennis des années 1930. Il s'en dégage beaucoup de charme, elle a une lithographie de grande qualité.

a GEORGE LEVY Motor cycle, 22cm (8.7in). The charming figures are very much in period. It was also available with a sidecar.

a GEORGE LEVY Motorrad, 22cm. Die hübschen Figuren entsprechen sehr dem Stil ihrer Zeit. Das Motorrad wurde auch als Seitenwagengespann hergestellt.

a GEORGE LEVY Motocyclette, 22cm. Ses charmantes figurines sont tout à fait de leur temps. Elle existait également avec side-car.

b TIPP & CO Motorcycle combination, 23.5cm (9.25in). This charming lithographed toy features a typical German family of the 1930s out for a ride.

b TIPP & CO Motorradgespann, 23,5cm. Dieses hübsche bedruckte Spielzeug stellt eine typische deutsche Familie der dreißiger Jahre bei einem Ausflug dar.

b TIPP & CO. Motocyclette à side car, 23,5cm. Ce charmant jouet lithographié représente une famille allemande typique des années 1930, en promenade.

a

b

c

c TIPP & CO Motor cycle, 22cm (8.7in). This features a rider and pillion passenger.

c TIPP & CO Motorrad, 22cm. Das Motorrad hat einen Fahrer und einen Sozius.

c TIPP & CO. Motocyclette, 22cm. Elle comprend un motocycliste et un passager à l'arrière.

d TIPP & CO Motorcycle and rider, 30cm (11.8in). This lithographed toy features a rider in a military style uniform.

d TIPP & CO Motorrad mit Fahrer, 30cm. Dieses bedruckte Spielzeug hat einen Fahrer in einer militär-ähnlichen Uniform.

d TIPP & CO. Motocycliste sur sa moto, 30cm. Ce jouet lithographié représente un motocycliste dans un uniforme de style militaire.

d

TIPP & CO "Christmas car", 31cm
12.2in). This features electric lights,
Father Christmas himself driving, and
an illuminated Christmas tree behind.
The car is a lithographed open two-
seater.

TIPP & CO „Weihnachtsauto", 31cm.
Der bedruckte offene Zweisitzer hat
elektrische Scheinwerfer und hinter
sich einen illuminierten Weihnachts-
baum. Der Fahrer ist ein Weihnachtsmann.

TIPP & CO. voiture de Noël, 31cm.
Cette voiture à éclairage électrique
est conduite par le père Noël en
personne, un arbre de Noël illuminé,
placé à l'arrière. La voiture est une
deux-places ouverte, lithographiée.